CIRCUS

EMBROIDERY

CIRCUS

EMBROIDERY

SUSIE JOHNS

CONTENTS

MOTIFS

PROJECTS

INTRODUCTION

For centuries we have been entertained and delighted by the circus. With trapeze artists and tumblers, jugglers, acrobats, magicians and animals, there is something for everyone.

This book of circus-themed embroidery designs includes animals, human performers and many other things associated with the Big Top. Circuses have gone through many transformations over the years and these days you are less likely to encounter exotic animals – but an embroidered circus is a fantasy and so you can include anything you wish.

The book is divided into three sections: at the beginning, there is a section to help you with materials, tools and basic stitches. It also includes guidance on how to prepare fabric, choose threads and use a hoop.

Then there are the motifs. These are provided as simple line drawings for you to trace straight from the page or photocopy, reducing or enlarging them as you please. Included is a stitched example of each motif to inspire you and to show how various stitches can be used and combined, but you can add your own details and variations.

Create a circus ground, complete with Big Top, ticket booth, tents and caravans; there's even a special train to transport the show from town to town. There are front-of-house staff to greet the audience and sell them a programme or some ice-cream, and circus crew to put up tents and look after the animals. The menagerie is stocked with big cats, elephants, horses and a whole array of other beasts. And then there are the performers: a troupe of talented artistes, including tightrope walkers, acrobats, tumblers, jugglers, magicians, dancers and, of course, clowns.

To complete the picture, you will find a selection of decorative borders, alphabets and numerals to combine with other motifs to make your own unique circus-themed designs.

Towards the end of the book, there is a selection of twelve projects, giving ideas on how to use the motifs to make gifts or embellish clothes. Each project is accompanied by step-by-step illustrations, helping to simplify the processes involved. Make a birthday card and a cake band for a circus-themed party; decorate your clothes with circus motifs; or make a brooch, a little purse, a mobile phone cover, needle case or a framed picture.

If you are new to embroidery, start with something straightforward, like a simple caravan or little tent outlined in backstitch or split stitch. From there you can progress to filling stitches and more elaborate patterns and colour schemes – a trapeze artist or a penguin, perhaps? When you are really confident, try a clown in a harlequin costume, or a strongman in a leopard-skin leotard – that will really test your embroidery skills.

Hand embroidery is a timeless craft that requires a good eye, a steady hand and very little in the way of equipment and materials. More than this, it is very absorbing and also very therapeutic. Use these simple skills to stitch some circus motifs. Use all the thread colours in your workbox to make them come to life. Roll up, roll up, ladies, gentlemen and children, and be inspired by the greatest show on earth!

BASIC EMBROIDERY KIT

Embroidery requires little in the way of basic tools and materials. Although you may want to add more specialized bits of kit later down the line, the items in this section cover everything you need to get started.

Fabric

For surface embroidery, you will need a plain-weave fabric. Cotton or linen are the best choices, with a smooth, tightly woven texture. Both cotton, which is relatively inexpensive, and linen, which costs a little more, are natural fabrics and the reason for choosing these is that the needle glides in and out more easily than it does with synthetic materials. To prove this for yourself, try out some sample stitches on a piece of pure cotton or linen and then try some on a poly-cotton.

PREPARING FABRIC

Natural fabrics, if not pre-shrunk, should be washed and ironed before you begin. It is a good idea to do this even if the finished item is something that will not need to be washed, as it makes most fabrics softer and easier to work with, allowing the needle to glide through easily.

Needles

Crewel needles

These are designed for embroidery, being of medium length with a sharp point and a long eye to accommodate several thicknesses of thread. You can use them for general sewing, too: the longer eye makes them easier to thread. They are available in sizes 1–12: the smaller the number, the finer the needle. Try to use a small needle rather than a large one, as it will be easier to push through the fabric. Your choice will be influenced by the number of thread strands you are using. As a guideline, a size 4 or 5 will accommodate two strands of stranded cotton; for three strands you will need a size 6 or 7.

Chenille needles

These are typically longer and thicker than crewel needles and useful for embroidery on heavier fabrics and with thicker threads.

Sharps

These needles have a small, round eye, and are useful for general sewing. Choose a longer needle length for tacking and gathering and a shorter length for stitching seams and hems. Shorter-length sharps are called 'betweens' and are a good choice for fine fabrics and tiny stitching. You will need a selection for making up the projects in this book – and you can use a sewing machine, if you have one, for some of the stages.

Thread

Embroidery threads

All the motifs in this book have been stitched using six-stranded embroidery thread. For the projects, DMC shade numbers are provided so you can match the colours exactly, if you wish.

Loosely wound in a skein, individual threads can be separated and then combined, so you can use any number of threads. Throughout this book, two strands have been used, which suits the scale of the motifs and the weight of the fabric – a medium-weight cotton sheeting. The only exception is the embroidered denim jacket on page 140 where, due to the heavier weight of the fabric, three strands have been used. To separate the strands, cut the required length of thread then fan out the strands at one end and pull out the number you require, one by one.

Sewing threads

When making up the various projects, whether sewing by hand or machine, it is a good idea to choose a thread with a fibre content that matches the fabric. For sewing natural fabrics, choose a mercerized cotton thread and for synthetic fabrics, use a polyester thread.

Try to match the colour of the fabric as closely as possible and if an exact match is not possible, choose a shade slightly darker. For tacking, choose a contrasting colour that shows up well against the fabric, making it easier to remove.

USING A NEEDLE THREADER

Threading a needle can be frustrating, so it is useful to own a needle threader. Push the wire loop through the eye of the needle, then pass the end of the thread through it. Pull the wire loop back through the eye of the needle, taking the thread through the eye. If you haven't got a needle threader, you can use a short length of thin wire or a small strip of thin paper folded in half.

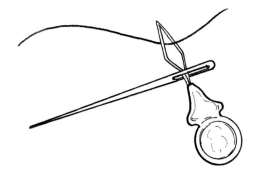

Embroidery hoops

Consisting of two wooden rings, the larger of which has a screw that can be tightened or loosened to accommodate fabrics of different weights, this holds the fabric taut, which is important when working stitches that might otherwise cause the fabric to pucker and distort. Plastic versions are also available, some of which have a spring clip instead of a screw.

As a general rule, stretching fabric in an embroidery hoop makes it easier to control the embroidery stitches and achieve an even tension. You can adjust each stitch as it is formed, making sure that it sits neatly on the surface of the fabric. This is particularly important when working satin stitch, because it is formed of fairly long strands that need to be of an even tension. Without a hoop, there is a tendency for the thread to be pulled too tightly and the fabric to become puckered.

Scissors

You will need a pair of embroidery scissors, which are small with sharp, pointed blades, essential for snipping threads and cutting away small areas of fabric. For cutting out fabric pieces, you will need a pair of good-quality dressmaking shears – which should be reserved for cutting only fabric, never paper – and a pair of all-purpose scissors for cutting paper and card when making templates. Scissors should be kept sharp. Pinking shears, with zigzag blades, are not essential but they come in useful for trimming the edges of fabrics that have a tendency to fray.

Markers

With most hand embroidery, you will need design lines marked on the fabric, as a guide to where to place the stitches. If the stitches will cover these lines completely – as in satin stitch, for example – the lines can be drawn with some kind of permanent marker. If, however, the stitches will be more open, and the design lines will show through, then the lines need to be drawn with a marker that will fade or that can be removed.

For permanent lines, there are permanent fabric marker pens available. A ballpoint pen (as opposed to a gel pen or rollerball) or an ordinary pencil can also be used. Before using one on a project, draw some marks on a scrap of fabric using your pen or pencil, then dampen the fabric and rub the marks with your fingertips, to make sure they do not smudge or run.

For making temporary marks on fabric, there are various pens and pencils available to buy. The ones that fade away by themselves are most useful for small areas of embroidery that are to be finished quite quickly, but you don't want the marks to fade before you have had a chance to finish the stitching.

Lines drawn with water-erasable markers will last longer and can be removed with water once the embroidery is complete. For small areas, to remove the pen marks, try rubbing them with a cotton bud dampened with cold water; for larger areas, you may need to immerse the fabric in water in order to remove the marks. Once again, it is wise to practise on a scrap of fabric first.

Some quilters' pencils and tailors' chalk pencils with a brush in the end can also be used and marks can be either rubbed or washed away. You can also buy special transfer pens and pencils that require heat to transfer drawn marks on to fabric. You will find guidelines on how to use these on page 12.

Iron

A steam iron is invaluable. When pressing an embroidered piece, keep a towel handy: fold it to provide a cushioned bed for the embroidery, place the embroidery right side down and cover with a pressing cloth. Press embroidered areas carefully to avoid squashing and flattening the stitches.

When making a project, pressing properly is as important as stitching: it helps to smooth out wrinkles, of course, but it also helps to shape fabric and set seams. Make sure your ironing board cover is clean, as dirt and scorch marks can be transferred to your fabric and spoil the appearance. When pressing delicate fabrics, always use a pressing cloth.

Other useful items

Buy good-quality steel pins that will not rust or become blunt. Keep them in a lidded box. Glass-headed pins are more expensive but very useful, as they are easier to see.

A tape measure is useful, and you'll also need a couple of rulers: a long one for drawing lines accurately and a small one for measuring small areas such as seam allowances. A T-square or set square is very useful for measuring neat right-angled corners.

A thimble is a useful accessory for some sewers, while others find it unnecessary or cumbersome.

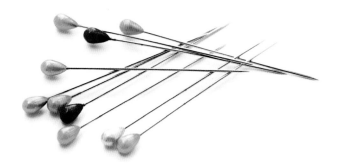

PREPARING TO SEW

Before you start stitching, there will be some preparation needed to make sure your designs, fabric and threads are ready.

~ Transferring designs ~

Here are two different methods that can be used for transferring the motif templates on to the fabric you wish to use. See page 11 for what type of marking pen or pencil to use.

Tracing

A lightweight fabric may be thin enough to lay on top of a design and trace the lines directly. With fabrics that are less translucent, you will find a light box useful, to make the lines of the design visible through the fabric. These days, light boxes are much smaller and more portable than they used to be. Instead of a cumbersome frame involving light bulbs, wires and bulky plugs, modern LED light boxes are really slim and have USB connections.

If you don't have a light box, however, you can improvise by taping the design to a window: tape the fabric on top and you should be able to see the design and trace it on to the fabric. With any direct tracing method, you will first need to trace or photocopy the design on to plain paper.

Heat transfer

An alternative to tracing is to make a heat transfer. For this, you will need a heat transfer pen or pencil – available from embroidery suppliers – and some thin white paper, such as layout or 'bank' paper (but not tracing paper, which will wrinkle under the heat of the iron).

One important thing to bear in mind when using this method is that your design will be reversed, so reverse your chosen motif or lettering when making your initial drawing.

1 Lay the paper over the design and trace it, using the special transfer pen or pencil.

2 Lay your fabric on an ironing board, lay the tracing face down on the fabric and carefully press with a hot iron, taking care that the paper's position doesn't shift or the transferred lines will be blurred. After the allotted time – and you should check the guidelines for your particular pen or pencil – you can lift off the paper to reveal the design on the fabric.

ENLARGING AND REDUCING MOTIFS

If you want your elephant to be larger than it appears on the page, or your sea lion to be smaller, you can easily do this by scanning the motifs on to a computer and altering the scale, or by using the reducing and enlarging facility on a photocopier.

Here is how to calculate the percentage.

To enlarge a motif
Measure the motif you wish to use, decide what size you want it to be, divide the finished size by the original size, and then multiply by 100 to achieve the percentage.

For example:
Original motif is 2in (5cm) high
You want it to be 5in (12.5cm) high
5 ÷ 2 = 2.5 x 100 = 250
You will need to photocopy the motif at 250%.

To reduce a motif
This is done in the same way as enlarging, but the numbers will be different and you will expect the calculated percentage to be less than 100.

For example:
Original motif is 5in (12.5cm) high
You want it to be 2in (5cm) high
2 ÷ 5= 0.4 x 100 = 40
You will need to photocopy the motif at 40%.

Preparing the fabric

First, press your fabric. Choose an embroidery hoop smaller than your piece of fabric. You will discover with practice what size of hoop feels most comfortable and practical for you. You may wish to see the whole design within the hoop or you may prefer to use a small hoop and move it to different areas of the design as you work.

Place your fabric on top of the plain ring of the embroidery hoop, then place the other part of the hoop – the one with the opening and the screw fitting – on top, pressing it down until the two parts of the ring align. You may have to loosen the screw in order for it to fit and, once in place, you will need to tighten the screw so that the fabric is firmly held in place.

Tug gently on the edges of the fabric so that it is nice and taut – but take care not to distort the fabric, as the grain should be kept straight.

The cut edges of the fabric are liable to fray, so you may wish to hem them or simply trim them with pinking shears.

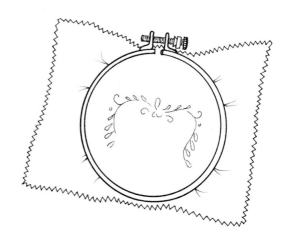

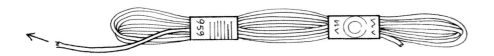

Preparing thread

Six-stranded embroidery thread is sold in skeins, held in place with two paper bands. Do not remove these bands but hold the skein in one hand and pull on the loose end to draw out a length of thread. Separate this length into the number of strands you wish to use – typically, one, two or three strands. Separate the strands by pulling them out individually. If you try to pull out more than one at a time, they will most likely tangle and knot together.

If your skein does become tangled, you may wish to wind the thread onto a bobbin. These are sold precisely for this purpose and are available made from card or plastic. You can keep a record of the thread shade number by writing it on the bobbin and bobbins can be stored in a box with a lid to keep them organized and dust free.

Starting to stitch

Thread your needle with the required number of strands of embroidery thread. Do not knot the end, as this can cause an unsightly lump or snag on the tip of your needle as you stitch. Instead, when you start a new piece of embroidery, leave about 1–2in (2.5–5cm) of thread loose on the wrong side of the fabric and work the first few stitches over it, so that it is secured in place. Trim off any excess thread tails. As you begin to sew with subsequent threads, these can be secured on the wrong side by running your needle under a group of stitches.

When stitching, you should insert your needle down into the fabric in a stabbing motion, then push it up again from below, rather than picking up a piece of fabric with the tip of your needle from the top of the work. This helps to maintain an even tension and keeps the fabric taut as you progress.

PREVENTING TANGLES

When sewing by hand, especially with embroidery stitches that involve twisting, looping and knotting, the thread has a tendency to become tangled and knotted.

To avoid this, try these tips:

* When threading your needle, use the free end of the thread from the skein or spool and make sure that the end you cut is the end that is secured to the fabric.

* Use a length of thread no longer than about 18in (45cm).

* As you sew, pull the needle in the direction in which you are sewing, usually from right to left.

* If the thread does become twisted, let go of the needle and allow it to dangle, so that the thread spins and untwists itself.

EMBROIDERY STITCHES

The style of stitching used in this book, known as surface embroidery, is like 'painting' with thread. The designs use only a handful of stitches to help keep things simple. Some are used for outlining and others for filling in areas so that the fabric beneath does not show through. Some stitches can be used for both and can create different textures and effects.

Running stitch

The most basic embroidery stitch is also one of the most versatile and popular. If you are working this stitch in a hoop, use a stabbing motion, taking the needle up through the fabric and pulling the thread taut before pushing it back down through the fabric, completing one stitch at a time. If you are working without a hoop, you can work several stitches at a time, taking the needle in and out of the fabric at a shallow angle, with a rocking motion. Running stitch can be used to outline shapes and can also be used as padding under satin stitch (see page 18), especially where a dark thread is used on a light-coloured fabric.

Working from right to left, bring the needle up to the surface, then back down into the fabric a little way along the stitch line and out again about the same distance along; repeat all along the line.

Backstitch

Backstitch can be used to stitch straight lines, wavy lines and curves. It is useful for outlining the edge of a shape and looks good in combination with most other embroidery stitches. In many of the motifs in the book, a single strand of thread is used to work outlines of backstitch, to emphasize shapes and to help define light-coloured areas that might not otherwise show up against the background fabric.

Working from right to left, bring the needle up through the fabric a little to the left of the beginning of the line to be worked, then back through at the beginning of the line and up again a stitch length in front of the place the needle first emerged. Repeat as needed.

Split stitch

As well as being a useful outlining stitch, rows of split stitch can be worked close together as a filling stitch.

1 Working from left to right, bring the needle up at the beginning of the line to be worked, then down a stitch length to the right.

2 Pull the thread through to form the first stitch, then bring the needle up through the centre of the stitch.

3 Repeat along the length of the line.

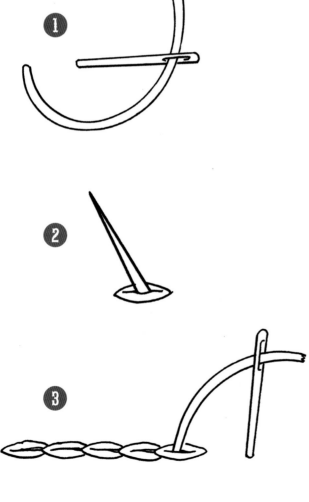

Stem stitch

As the name implies, this stitch is useful for stitching stems. It also makes a good, solid outline.

Working from left to right, bring the needle up, then down a stitch length to the right. Pull the thread through to form the first stitch. Bring the needle up just above the centre of the first stitch and along the line, to the right, another stitch length. Repeat. You can vary the length of the stitches and the slant, to make a thinner or thicker line.

Chain stitch

Cleverly linked stitches create a line that resembles a chain. This is a versatile stitch that can be used to form straight or curved lines. Rows of chain stitch can also be worked close together as a filling.

1 Working in whichever direction is most comfortable, bring the needle up, then back down at the same point and out again a stitch length along the line, with the tip of the needle under the loop of thread.

2 Pull the thread through to form the first stitch, then take the needle back down through the loop of the first stitch and out again a stitch length along the line, with the tip of the needle under the loop of thread once again. Repeat, to create a chain of linked loops.

Long-and-short stitch

This variation of satin stitch can be used to cover larger shapes. It can be worked in several colours or in different shades of the same colour.

Draw an outline of the shape to be filled and take the needle in and out of the fabric just outside the outline, so that the stitches cover it. Work the first row in alternating long and short stitches. Work the second and subsequent rows in stitches that are all the same length, taking the needle into the end of the stitch above, so that alternate stitches will be offset, or 'stepped'.

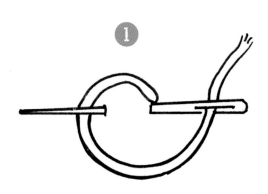

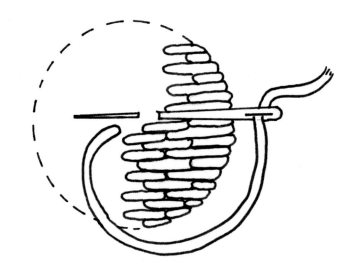

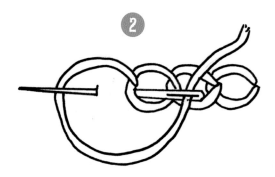

Satin stitch

This stitch should be close together and parallel, with no gaps, in order to create a solid area of colour. Keep stitches quite short so that they do not snag or pull, so make sure that shapes to be filled are quite small. For larger shapes, use long-and-short stitch instead.

It can also be worked at a slant. For some shapes, instead of starting at one end, you may find it easier to start in the centre and work outwards, in two stages. This can help to keep the stitches parallel.

When working with a dark-coloured thread on a light-coloured fabric, you may wish to pre-fill the inside of the shape first with rows of running stitch in the same coloured thread. Work the running stitches in a different direction from the satin stitches.

1 Draw an outline of the shape to be filled. Working from right to left, or from bottom to top if you find it easier, bring the needle up on the right-hand side of the shape, just outside the drawn line, then down into the fabric on the left, also outside the line. Pull the thread through. Bring the needle back out on the right-hand side of the shape, next to the first stitch.

2 Repeat this process, keeping your stitches close together and covering the drawn outline.

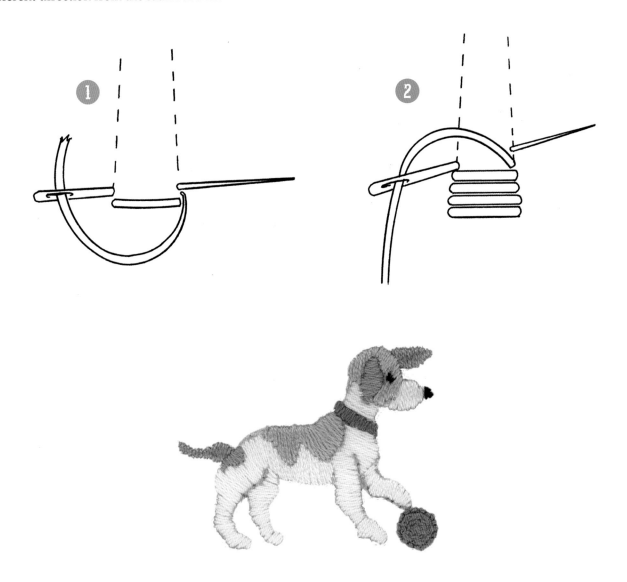

French knots

The French knot is a decorative stitch that forms a raised spot on the fabric. On small-scale motifs it is useful to denote buttons, eyes or spots.

1 Bring the needle through to the right side of the fabric. Hold the thread close to the surface of the fabric and wrap it around the needle twice.

2 Pull the thread tight and re-insert the needle close to where it emerged. Keeping the tension on the wrapped thread, pull the needle through to the back of the work.

3 The knot that is formed should sit on the surface of the fabric.

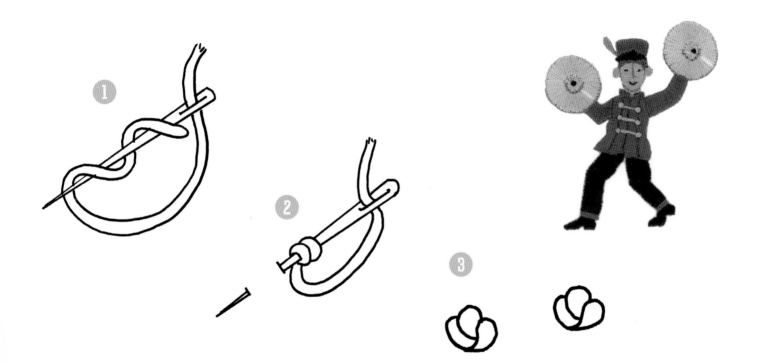

FASTENING OFF

To fasten off a thread, make sure you have about 4in (10cm) of thread remaining; any shorter than this and it will be difficult to manoeuvre the needle. Do not simply cut off the thread but run the needle under a few stitches first, to secure the end before trimming.

Try not to leave lots of loose ends on the back of your work. Trim them off close to the fabric, after securing. This is particularly important when working on light-coloured fabrics, as any stray ends may be visible through the fabric and will spoil the appearance.

FINISHING TECHNIQUES

Once you've worked your embroidery and made up the project following the instructions, there are a few useful finishing techniques that you need to know.

∽ Slipstitching ∽

When making some of the projects, you will need to join the folded edges of two pieces of fabric. Use slipstitch for this.

Fold in the raw edges on each side of the gap, then secure the thread under one of the folds, where it won't be seen. Use the tip of the needle to pick up a small section of fabric along the fold on one side. Then pick up a small amount of fabric on the fold on the other side. Pull the thread to close the gap. Repeat all along and fasten off neatly. If you execute slipstitch properly, the stitches should be indiscernible.

∽ Oversewing ∽

Sometimes, instead of slipstitching, oversewing – or whipstitch – is preferable. This means that you take your needle through both folds, as before, but you don't attempt to hide the stitches in the folds. This method is used on the bias binding ties of the baby bib on page 116.

Fold in the raw edges and place the two pieces of fabric with wrong sides together and folded edges aligned. Take the needle through all layers from back to front. Repeat, taking the needle from back to front each time.

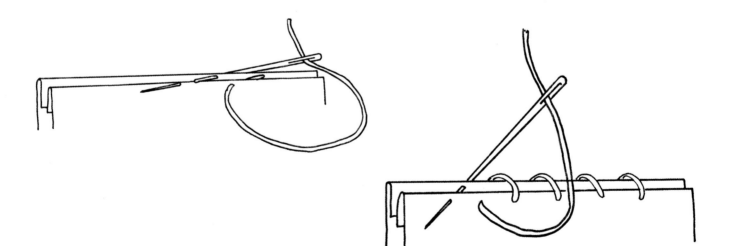

Binding

When binding an uneven edge, a corner or curve, do this in two stages.

1 First, open out the binding and line up one raw edge with the edge of the fabric. Stitch along the fold line by hand or machine.

2 Second, fold the binding over to enclose the raw edge of the fabric, and slipstitch the other long folded edge of the binding in place.

Topstitching

Topstitching creates a crisp finish and holds layers of fabric neatly and securely in place. It is used on the Clown Purse on page 106, where lines of topstitching run parallel to the zip.

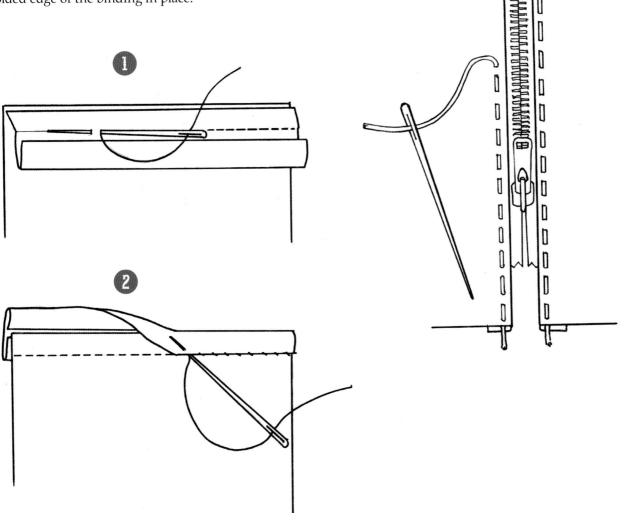

We are proud to present

THE MOST MAGNIFICENT

MOTIFS

Make
MAGIC WITH THREAD

CIRCUS SIGNS

 TENTS AND TICKET OFFICE

 **TRAIN**

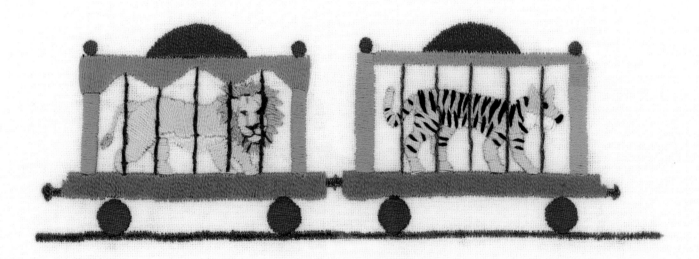

★ CARAVANS AND TRAILERS

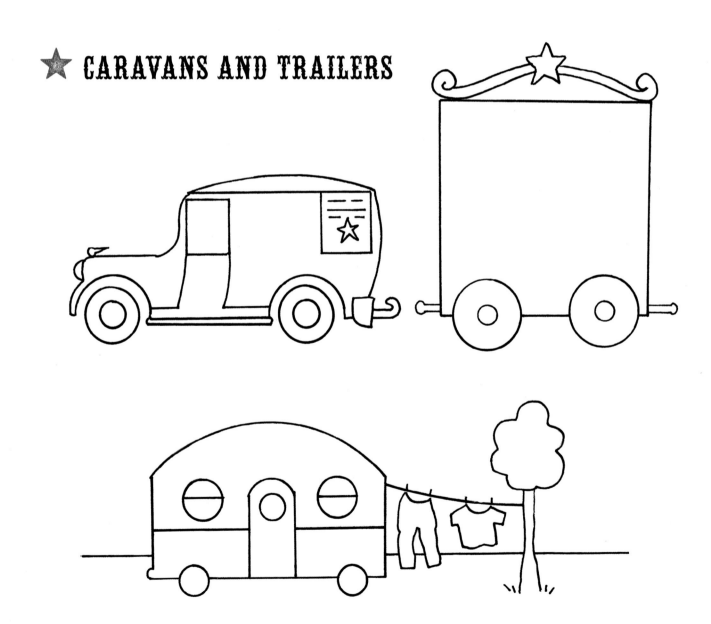

SEA LIONS

⭐ **PENGUINS**

⭐ **DOGS**

★ BIG CATS

★ BEARS

★ HORSES

★ ELEPHANTS AND BIRDS

EXOTIC ANIMALS

★ **MONKEYS**

★ **RINGMASTERS**

STRONGMEN
AND STRONGWOMEN

★ ACROBATS

BALANCING ACTS

★ TIGHTROPE WALKERS

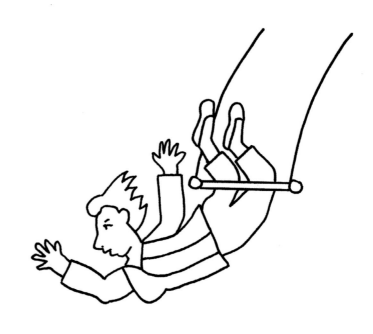

⭐ **TRAPEZE ARTISTS**

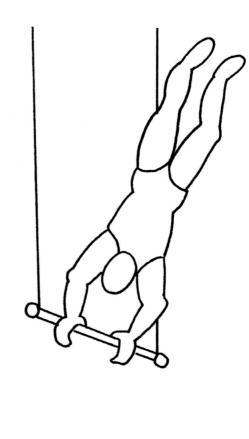

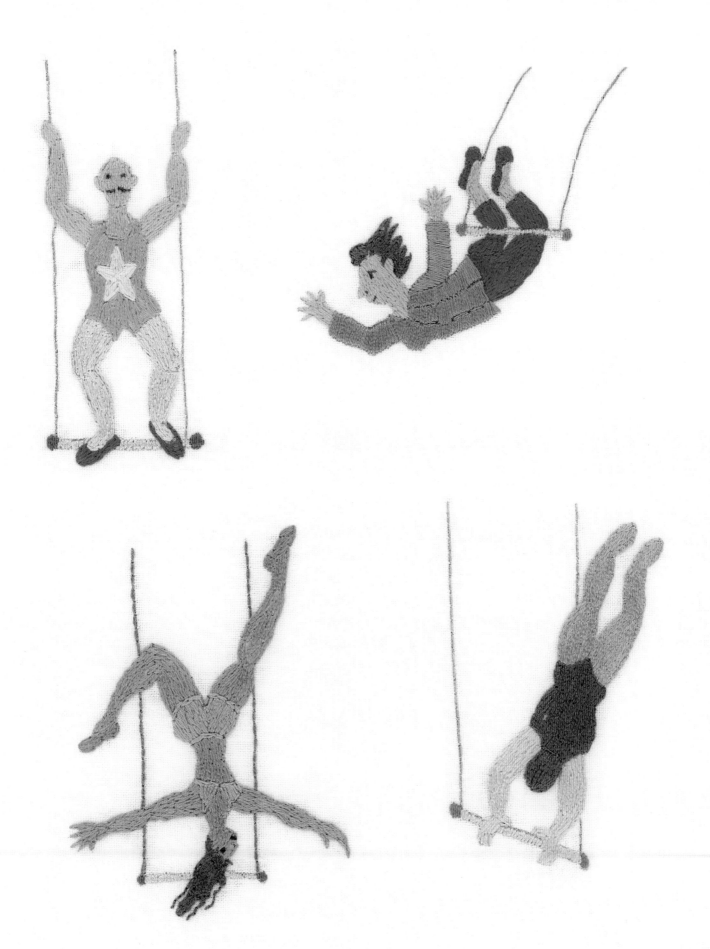

CLOWNS

★ CLOWNS

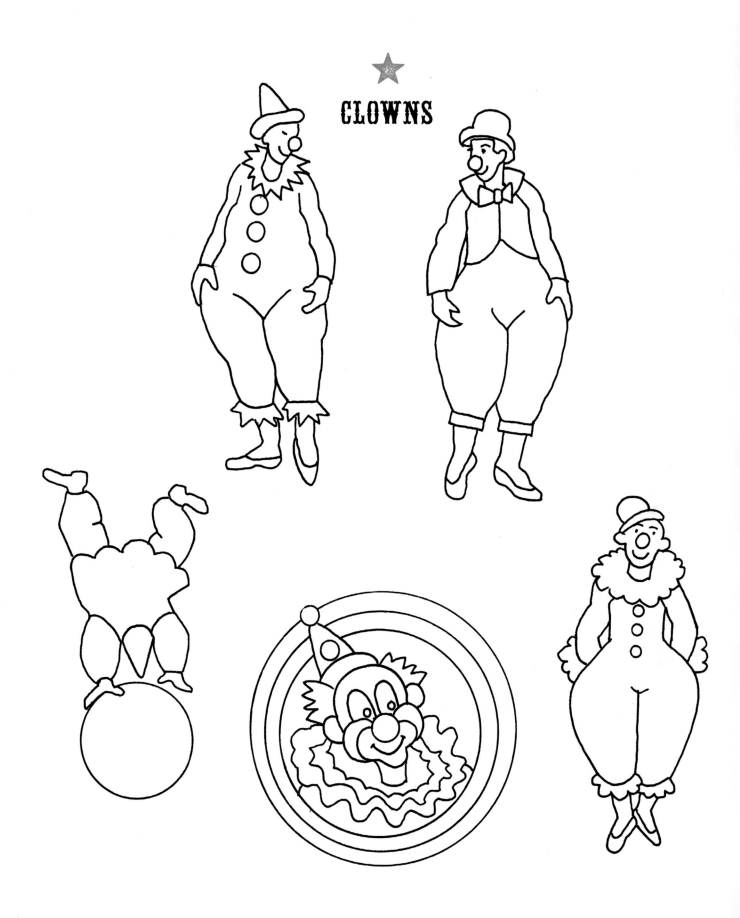

★ JUGGLERS

★ MAGIC ACTS

★ DANCERS

★ **ANIMAL TAMERS**

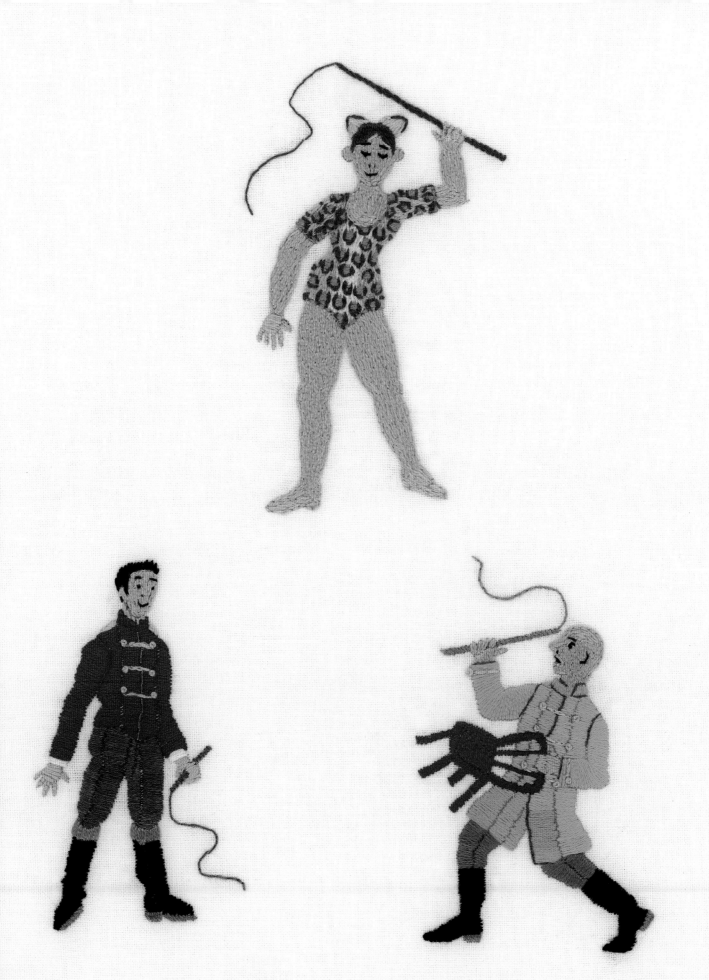

★ **MUSICIANS**

FRONT OF HOUSE

★ CREW

★ BOXES

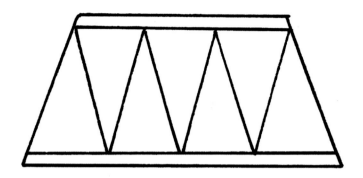

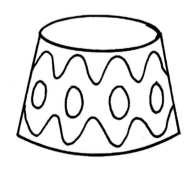  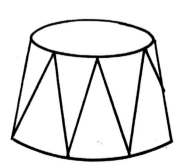

BANNERS AND FRAMES

★ DECORATIVE BORDERS

A B C D E
F G H I J
K L M N O
P Q R S T
U V W X Y
Z

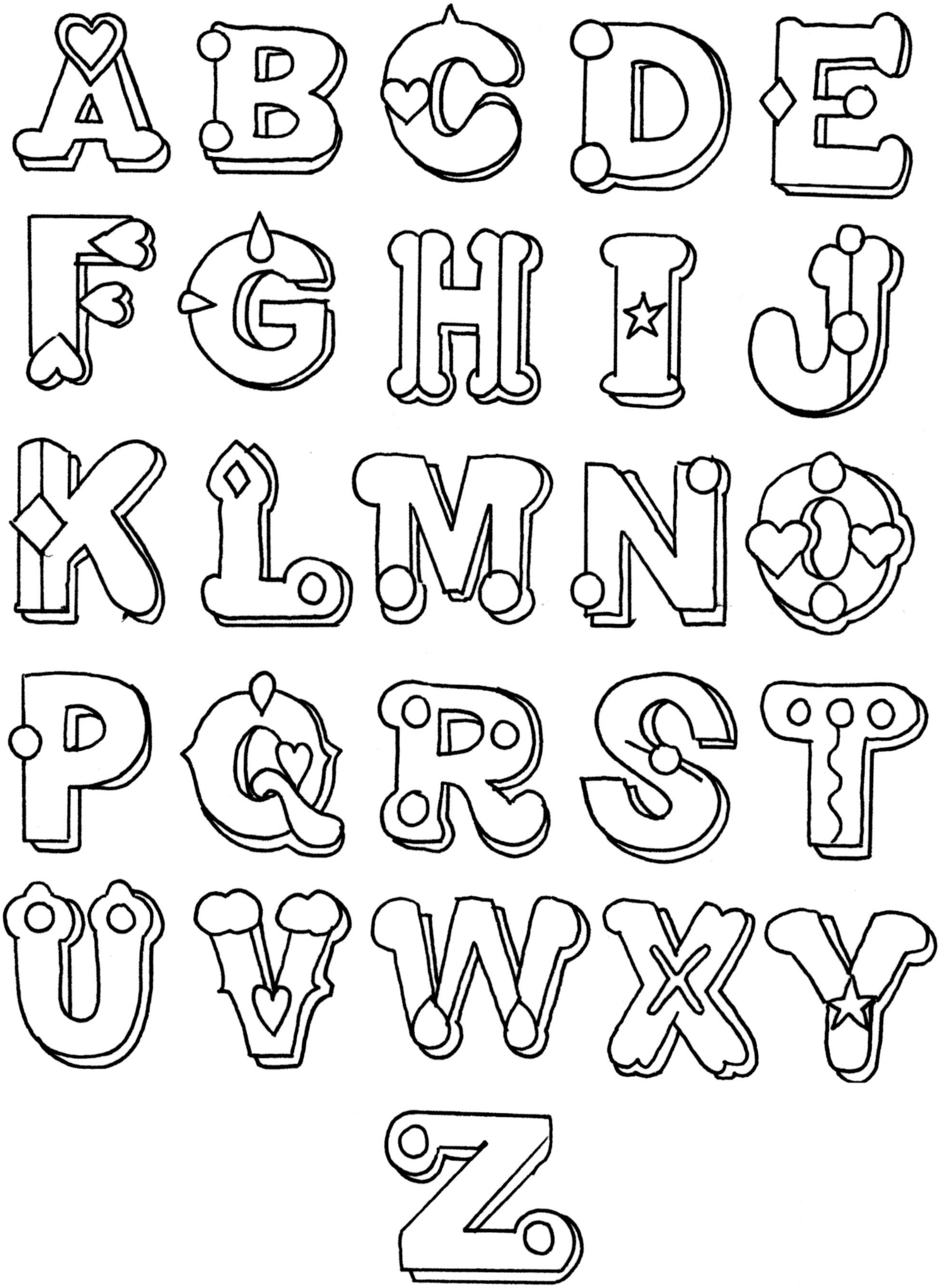

CIRCUS

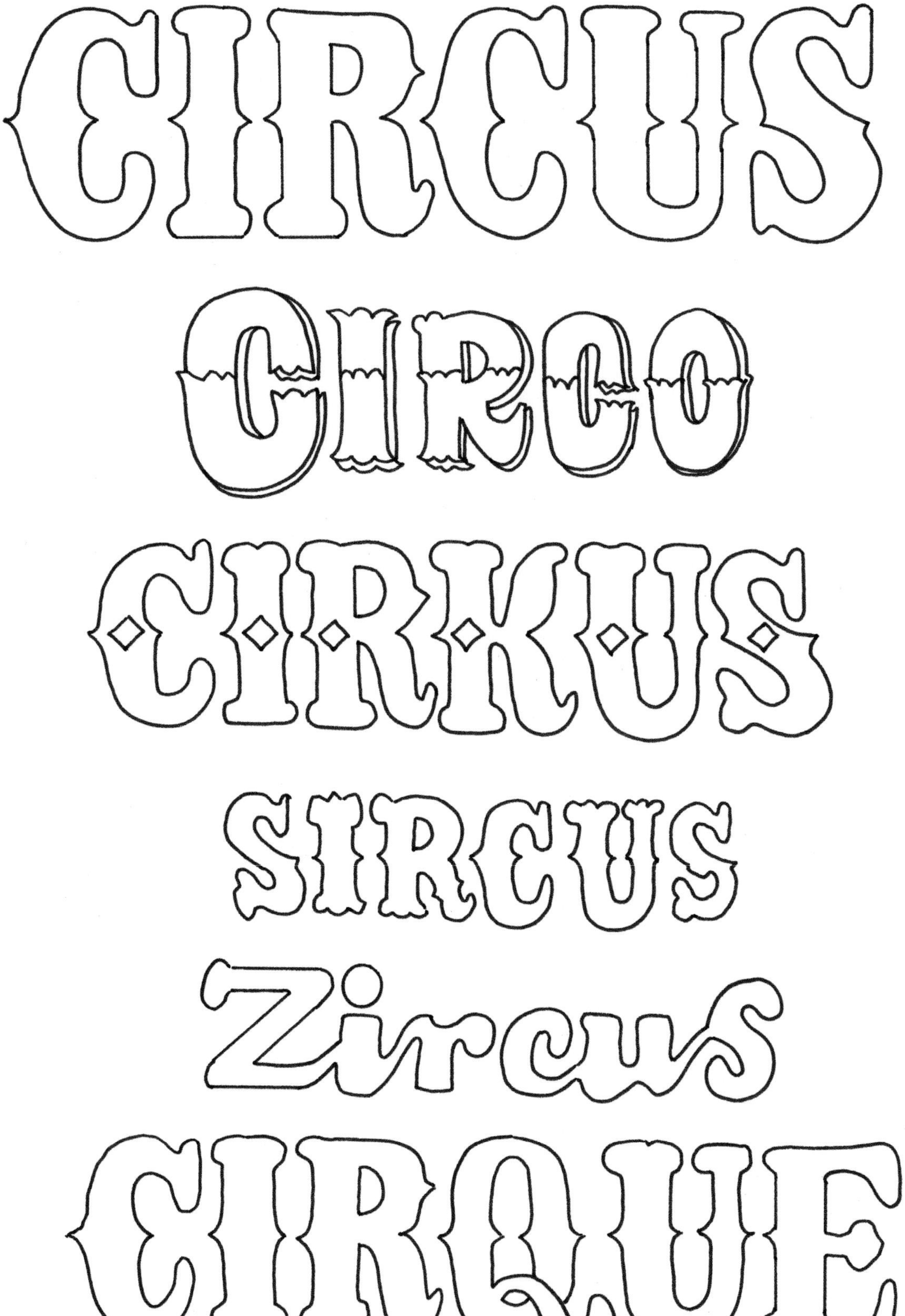

CIRCO

CIRKUS

SIRCUS

Zircus

CIRQUE

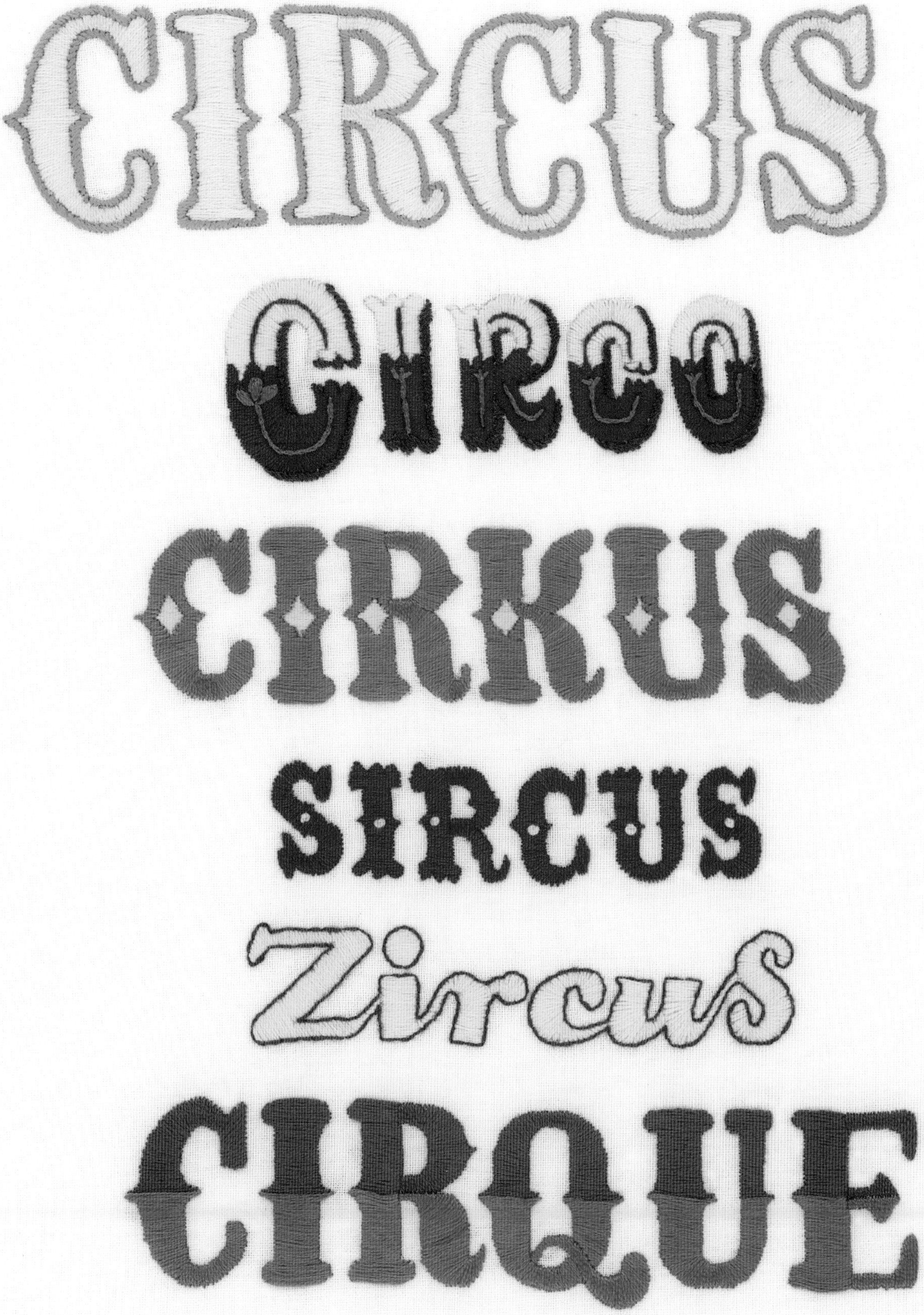

CIRCUS

CIRCO

CIRKUS

SIRCUS

Zircus

CIRQUE

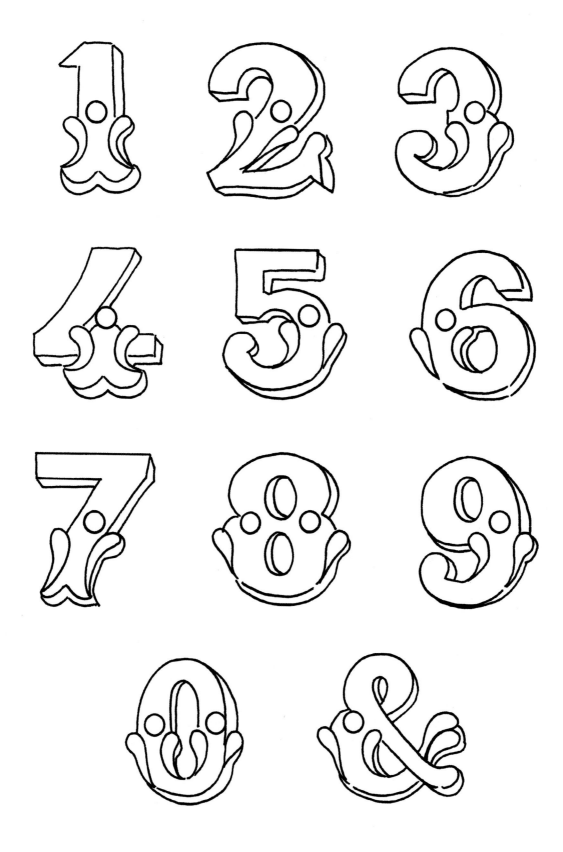

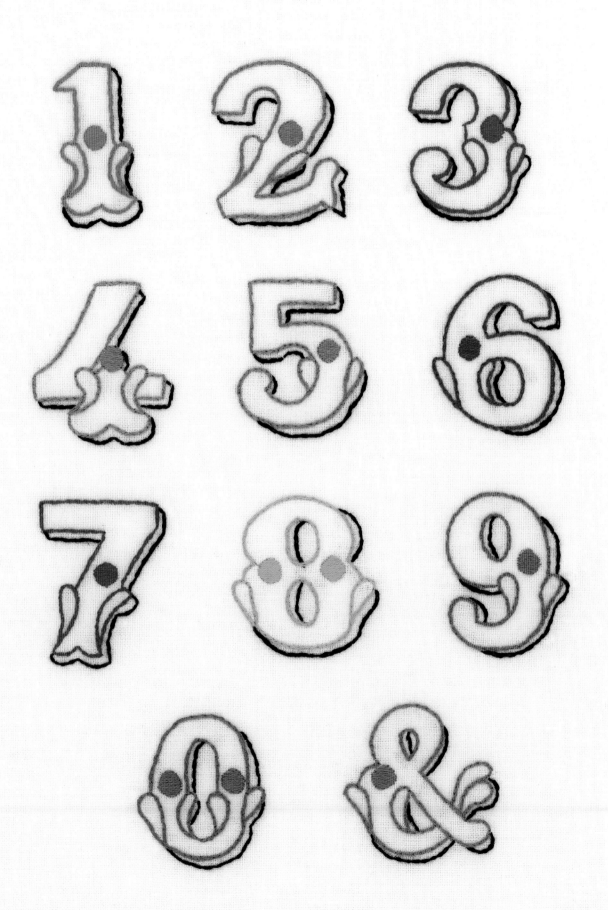

We are proud to present

OUR LEGENDARY

PROJECTS

The Most
MARVELLOUS
THINGS TO MAKE

SEA LION BIRTHDAY CARD

This card features a sea lion cleverly balancing three balls, for a third birthday. It would be easy to adjust the design to show other numbers and increase or decrease the number of balls. If there are too many balls to fit on the sea lion's nose, place them on the surrounding floor.

YOU WILL NEED

★ White cotton or linen fabric, at least 8 x 6in (20 x 15cm)
★ Lightweight wadding, 3³/₈ x 2⁷/₈in (8.5 x 7.5cm)
★ DMC six-stranded embroidery thread in the following colours: 666 red, 726 daffodil, 844 dark grey, 996 turquoise, blanc
★ Medium-weight card
★ Washi tape, approximately ¼in (6mm) wide, in two colours
★ Basic embroidery kit (see pages 8–11)
★ 5in (12.5cm) embroidery hoop
★ Craft knife
★ Cutting mat
★ Double-sided tape
★ Fabric glue (optional)

666 red

726 daffodil

844 dark grey

996 turquoise

blanc

FINISHED SIZE

5¹/₂ x 6¹/₄in (14 x 16cm)

Use two strands of embroidery thread throughout, apart from the sea lion's whiskers.

On white cotton or linen fabric, using an erasable marker pen, mark out a rectangle measuring 4 3/4 x 5in (12 x 13cm). Do not cut it out at this stage. Photocopy the sea lion motif from page 32, reducing it in size to approximately 2in (5cm) tall, including the box (see page 13). Photocopy your chosen numeral from page 94, reducing it in size to approximately 1 1/2 in (4cm) tall. Transfer the motifs on to your fabric (see page 12), making sure they sit within the marked rectangle. Add the appropriate number of circles, to represent balls. Make sure that the overall design area is no larger than 3 1/2 in (8.5cm) tall and 3in (7.5cm) wide. Place the fabric in a 5in (12.5cm) embroidery hoop; using a hoop this size means that the whole motif will fit inside the circle.

With 844 dark grey, embroider the whole sea lion in split stitch (see page 16). Using a single strand of the same colour, embroider the whiskers in backstitch (see page 15). Using blanc, add a few short lines of split stitch on the body and tail, to suggest highlights, and create an eye with a single French knot (see page 19). Using 666 red and satin stitch (see page 18), fill the box, balls and the single red line indicating the floor.

Embroider the numeral in satin stitch, using 666 red, 726 daffodil and 996 turquoise, and referring to the photograph of the finished card for the colour placement. Using 844 dark grey and satin stitch, fill in the drop shadow around the number.

Remove the fabric from the hoop and press on the reverse, following the pressing guidelines on page 11. Cut out the rectangle of fabric along the lines you have drawn.

1 Using a craft knife and a cutting mat, measure and cut out a 16 1/2 x 6 1/4 in (42 x 16cm) rectangle from the card. In the centre of the card, mark out a rectangle 3 1/2 in (9cm) high and 3 1/8 in (8cm) wide: the top of this rectangle should be 1 1/4 in (3cm) from the top edge of the card. Cut it out to create an aperture. Measure and draw two vertical lines all the way down the card, each 5 1/2 in (14cm) from the short edges. Place a ruler on each line in turn and lightly score along the lines to make it easier and neater to fold the card.

2 Trim a very thin sliver from the left-hand edge so that, when you fold the left-hand section inwards across the centre, this edge will not quite meet the other fold, ensuring a neat fit. Apply double-sided tape all around the aperture on the inside of the card and peel off the backing paper.

3 Place the embroidered fabric face down on the card so that it covers the aperture and the whole of the embroidered design is visible. Press to stick down the edges. Place the wadding centrally on top of the embroidery: it should be slightly smaller than the aperture. Apply fabric glue or more double-sided tape all round the edges of the fabric, right to the top and bottom edges of the middle section and right up to the two folds, then fold over the left-hand section of card and press down to stick it firmly in place.

4 On the right side of the card, to create a border, stick lengths of washi tape slightly longer than the aperture, so that the strips overlap where they intersect at each corner. Using a craft knife, make a small diagonal cut through the double thickness of tape at each corner, taking care not to cut through the card, then peel away and discard the excess tape. Press the corners of the tape to the card, to form a neat mitre. Repeat with a contrast tape for a double border.

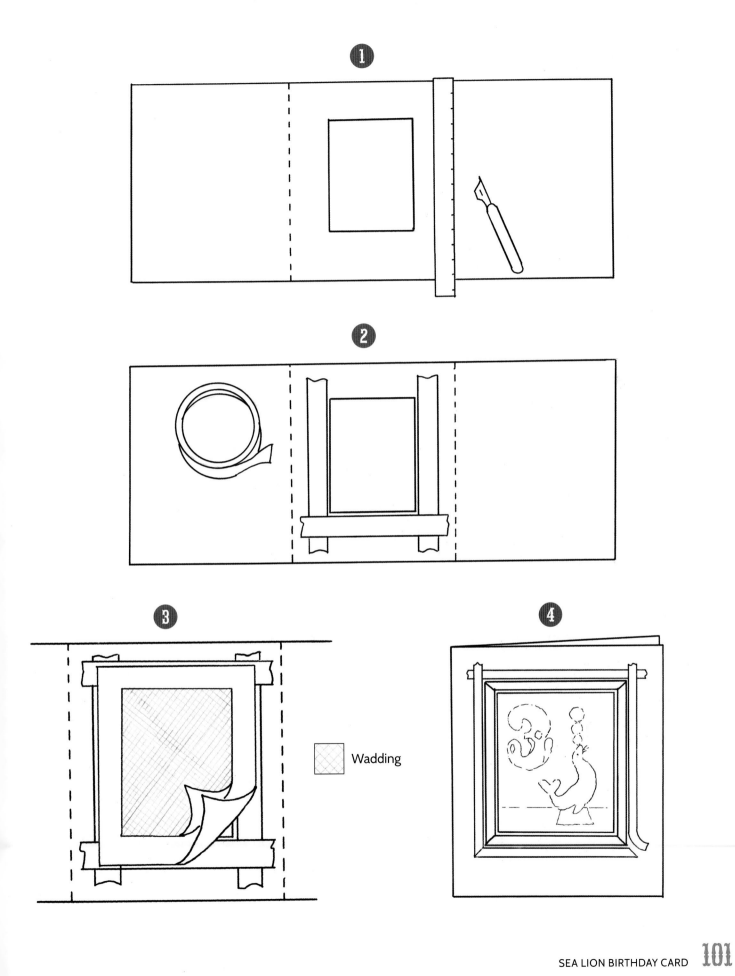

Wadding

MONOGRAM BADGE

A single letter of the alphabet, embroidered in bright colours, makes a lovely badge. Easy and quick to do, you could make a number of them, with different letters, as gifts or party favours for a circus-themed party — one for each circus star and maybe a larger one for the ringmaster.

YOU WILL NEED

★ White cotton or linen fabric, at least 6in (15cm) square
★ Lightweight wadding, small scrap
★ Felt, small scrap
★ DMC six-stranded embroidery thread in the following colours: 310 black, 444 golden yellow, 996 turquoise
★ White sewing thread
★ Flat button, 1³/₄in (4.5cm) in diameter
★ Small glass beads in assorted colours, approximately 60
★ Basic embroidery kit (see pages 8–11)
★ 4in (10cm) embroidery hoop
★ Beading needle
★ Brooch pin

■ 310 black

444 golden yellow

996 turquoise

FINISHED SIZE

1³/₄in (4.5cm)

EMBROIDERING THE ALPHABET LETTER

Use two strands of embroidery thread throughout.

Photocopy your chosen letter from the alphabet on page 90. Make any alterations you wish: in this example, two stars were added, one on each upright part of the 'H'. Transfer the letter onto the fabric (see page 12), placing it centrally. Place the fabric in a 4in (10cm) embroidery hoop.

With 444 golden yellow, embroider the two stars in satin stitch (see page 18). Embroider each point of the star separately, starting at the point and working towards the centre. Fill in the rest of the letter in satin stitch, using 996 turquoise. Using 310 black and satin stitch, fill in the drop shadow around the letter.

Remove the fabric from the hoop and press on the reverse, following the pressing guidelines on page 11.

MAKING THE BADGE

1 Draw a circle 3³/4in (9.5cm) in diameter on the fabric, making sure the embroidered letter is in the centre. Cut out along the outline you have drawn. Thread your needle with two strands of white sewing thread. Work a line of running stitch (see page 15) around the perimeter of the fabric, about ¹/8in (3mm) from the edge.

2 Measure, draw and cut out a circle of wadding 1³/4in (4.5cm) in diameter, using the button as a template. Cut out a circle of felt the same size for the back of the badge, and put it to one side.

3 Place the fabric right side down, with the wadding centred on top and the button on top of the wadding. Pull up the thread ends to gather, and secure the ends firmly.

4 Stitch the brooch pin to the circle of felt, placing it just above the centre. Place the felt centrally on the back of the badge and slipstitch the edges of the felt to the fabric (see page 20).

5 Using white thread and a beading needle, sew beads one by one around the perimeter of the badge.

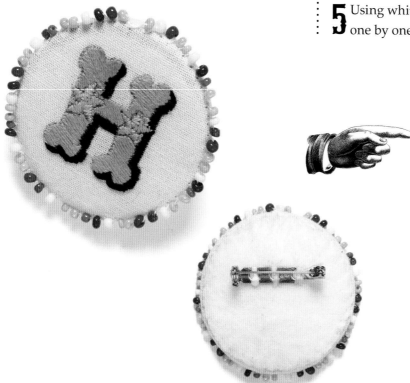

If you haven't got a button of the exact dimensions given here, choose one slightly smaller or larger – just check that it is wide enough to accommodate the embroidered letter.

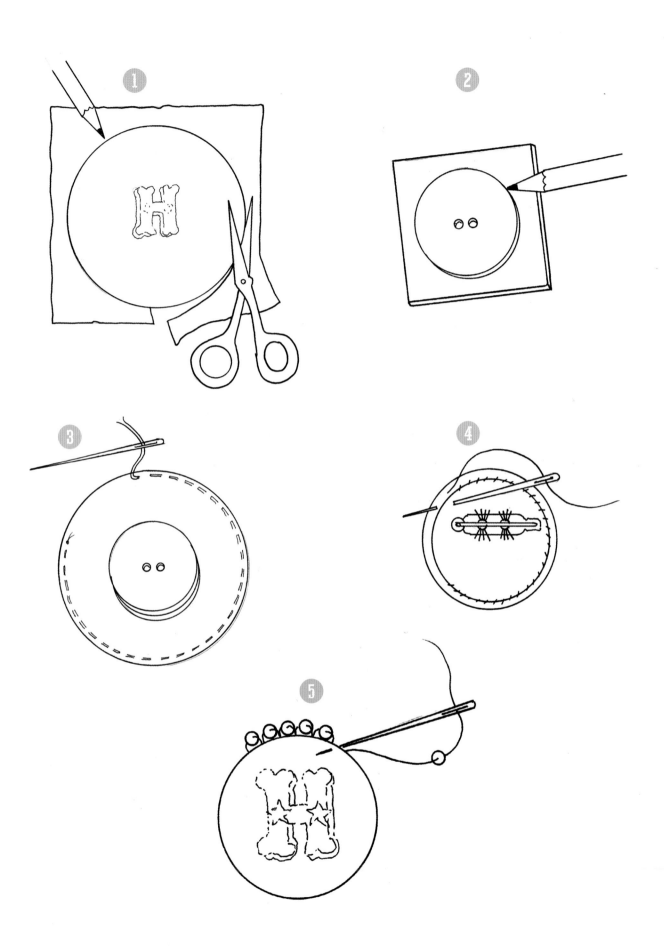

CLOWN PURSE

This little zipped purse is the perfect carrying case for all sorts of odds and ends. Its size and shape makes it handy for headphones, coins, a small mirror or compact — or maybe a spare red nose for when you feel like dressing up as a clown!

YOU WILL NEED

★ White cotton or linen fabric, approximately 6in (15cm) square
★ Printed cotton fabric, at least 5in (12.5cm) square
★ Two pieces of plain cotton fabric, each at least 5in (12.5cm) square, for lining
★ DMC six-stranded embroidery thread in the following colours: 310 black, 333 blue violet, 606 scarlet, 740 orange, 977 light tan, 3609 mauve pink, 3845 cyan, blanc
★ Sewing thread to match the fabric
★ Nylon zip, at least 6in (15cm) long
★ Basic embroidery kit (see pages 8–11)
★ 5in (12.5cm) embroidery hoop

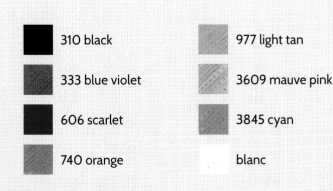

■	310 black	▨	977 light tan
▨	333 blue violet	▨	3609 mauve pink
■	606 scarlet	▨	3845 cyan
▨	740 orange	□	blanc

FINISHED SIZE

Approximately 4in (10cm) in diameter

EMBROIDERING THE CLOWN

Use two strands of embroidery thread throughout, unless otherwise stated.

On the white cotton, mark out a circle 4³/4in (12cm) in diameter using a pencil or ballpoint pen. Photocopy the clown motif from page 64. Using a water-soluble marker pen, transfer the motif onto the fabric (see page 12), placing it centrally within the circle. Place the fabric in a 5in (12.5cm) embroidery hoop.

Thread your needle with two strands of 606 scarlet and fill in the nose with satin stitch (see page 18). Then, using two strands of blanc, fill in the eyes, large mouth shape and the hat. Using two strands of 977 light tan, fill in the face using satin stitch and the neck using long-and-short stitch (see page 17). Using 333 blue violet, stitch the pompoms on the hat, with straight stitches radiating out from the centre. Then use the blue violet and 3609 mauve pink to fill in the layers of the neck ruff in satin stitch. Below this, work wide satin stitch stripes in 740 orange and narrow stripes in between using mauve pink. Use the orange thread for the hair. Using two strands of 310 black, fill in the inner circle that frames the clown, then with 3845 cyan fill in the outer ring, both in satin stitch.

With two strands of 606 scarlet, embroider a smiling mouth in split stitch (see page 16) on top of the white mouth shape. With 3845 cyan, embroider French knots (see page 19) for the eyes. Use two strands of black to stitch the eyebrows in split stitch, then use a single strand for outlining the hat, around the ears, around the neck and under the nose and chin.

Remove the fabric from the hoop and wash out the erasable pen lines using cold water (see page 11). Leave to dry. Press the fabric on the reverse, following the pressing guidelines on page 11.

MAKING THE PURSE

1 Cut out the embroidered circle along the lines you have drawn. Cut one circle the same size from the patterned fabric and two from the plain fabric. Then cut the patterned fabric circle and one of the plain fabric circles in half, making sure the cuts follow the straight grain of the fabric.

2 Place one of the plain semicircles right side up, with the zip right side up on top and one of the patterned semicircles right side down on top of the zip. The curved edges of the semicircles should be aligned and the straight edges about ¹/8in (3mm) in from the edge of the zip. Stitch through all thicknesses by hand or machine, ¹/4in (6mm) from the fabric edges. Repeat the process on the other side of the zip with the other two semicircles.

3 Fold the fabric pieces away from the zip and press, again aligning the edges of the semicircles, then topstitch (see page 21) along the straight edge of each semicircle, as close to the fold as possible.

4 Partially open the zip. Close the gap between the tapes on the open end with a few stitches. With this part of the case – the back – right way up, place the embroidered circle face down on top and the remaining plain fabric circle right side up on top of this. Pin the layers together, then stitch all round with a ³/8in (1cm) seam allowance

5 Cut off the ends of the zip level with the edges of the fabric. Snip into the seam allowance all round, then turn the purse right side out through the open zip.

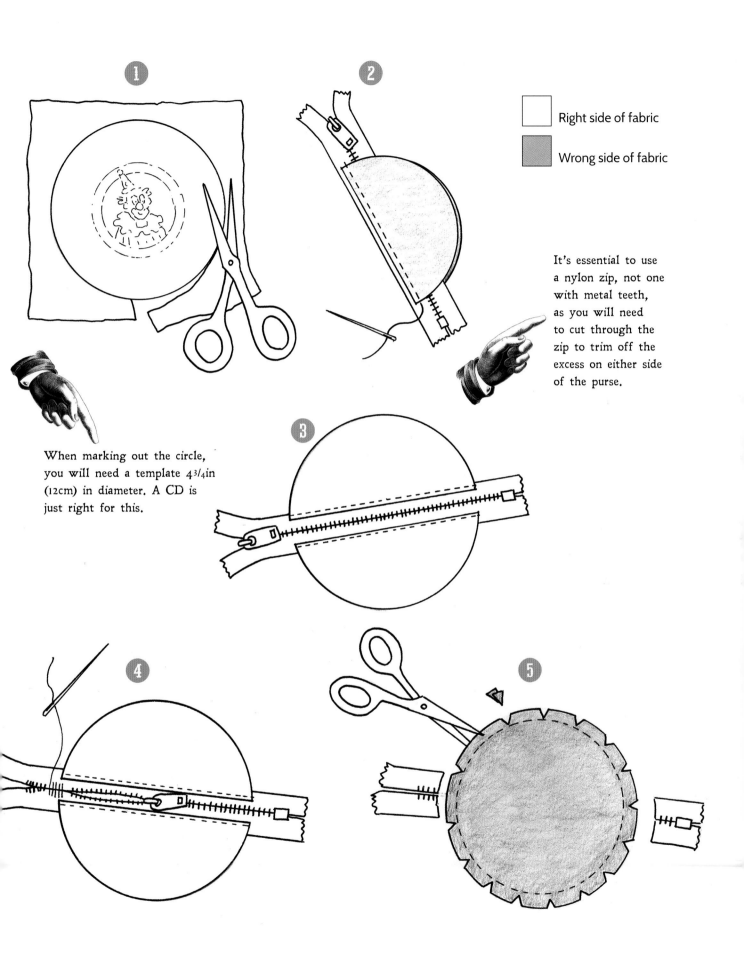

It's essential to use a nylon zip, not one with metal teeth, as you will need to cut through the zip to trim off the excess on either side of the purse.

Right side of fabric

Wrong side of fabric

When marking out the circle, you will need a template 4³/4in (12cm) in diameter. A CD is just right for this.

CIRCUS BAND PHONE CASE

A slipcover is a good way to protect your mobile phone from scratches. This one features an embroidered musician – the clarinettist from the circus band, resplendent in his smart uniform with gold braid. Why not choose a ringtone to match? Try 'Entry of the Gladiators'!

YOU WILL NEED

★ White cotton or linen fabric, approximately 6in (15cm) square
★ Printed cotton fabric, 6³/₄ x 4¹/₄in (17 x 11cm), for backing
★ Two pieces of plain cotton fabric, each 6³/₄ x 4¹/₄in (17 x 11cm), for lining
★ DMC six-stranded embroidery thread in the following colours: 310 black, 444 golden yellow, 642 elephant grey, 740 orange, 977 light tan, 995 aqua
★ Sewing thread to match the fabric
★ Basic embroidery kit (see pages 8–11)
★ 5in (12.5cm) embroidery hoop

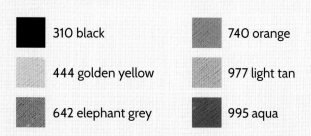

■ 310 black

■ 444 golden yellow

■ 642 elephant grey

▨ 740 orange

▨ 977 light tan

■ 995 aqua

FINISHED SIZE

Approximately 6 x 3³/₄in (15 x 9.5cm)

The measurements given here will comfortably fit a mobile phone measuring 5¹/₂ x 2³/₄in (14 x 7cm). If your phone has different dimensions, calculate the size of each of the main pieces of fabric and the lining pieces by adding 1¹/₂in (4cm) to the width and 1¹/₄in (3cm) to the length of the phone.

EMBROIDERING THE MUSICIAN

Use two strands of embroidery thread throughout, unless otherwise stated.

On the white cotton, mark out a 6³/₄ x 4¹/₄in (17 x 11cm) rectangle, using a pencil or a ballpoint pen. Photocopy the musician from page 76 and add a few musical notes. Using a water-soluble marker pen, transfer the motif onto the fabric (see page 12), placing it centrally within the rectangle. Place the fabric in a 5in (12.5cm) embroidery hoop.

Thread your needle with 995 aqua and embroider the uniform, including the hat, in satin stitch (see page 18). Work the stitches horizontally on the trousers and on the panels of the jacket. On the sleeves, work stitches across the width of the sleeve, fanning out the stitches where the elbow bends so that they follow the contour of the arm. Using 444 golden yellow, work the braids across the chest, on the cuff and on the shoulder in chain stitch (see page 17), keeping the stitches small, neat and evenly spaced. Work the braid up the side of the trouser leg in a similar way, using 740 orange. With the same colour, fill in the feather on the hat in satin stitch.

Fill in the face and hand in satin stitch, using 977 light tan. Embroider the clarinet, the hat peak and the shoes in satin stitch, using 310 black. Fill in the mouthpiece of the clarinet and the hair in satin stitch, using 642 elephant grey.

Use a single strand of black to stitch the musical notes and the eye, eyebrow and mouth. For short straight lines a single small stitch will suffice. French knots (see page 19) will create small neat dots.

Remove the fabric from the hoop and wash out the erasable pen lines using cold water (see page 11). Leave to dry. Press on the reverse, following the pressing guidelines on page 11.

MAKING THE PHONE SLEEVE

1 Cut out the embroidered fabric rectangle along the lines you have drawn. Place the embroidered fabric, which will form the front of the case, and the backing fabric right sides together. Pin, then stitch by hand or machine along both sides and across the bottom, with a ¹/₄in (6mm) seam allowance. Do the same with the two lining pieces, but with a ³/₈in (1cm) seam allowance on the two long edges.

2 Cut across the corners: this helps to reduce the bulk when the case is turned right side out.

3 On both the outer case and the lining, turn ³/₈in (1cm) to the wrong side along the top edge and press. Turn the outer case right side out.

4 Slide the lining inside the case, aligning the seams. Slipstitch the lining to the case with small, neat stitches (see page 20).

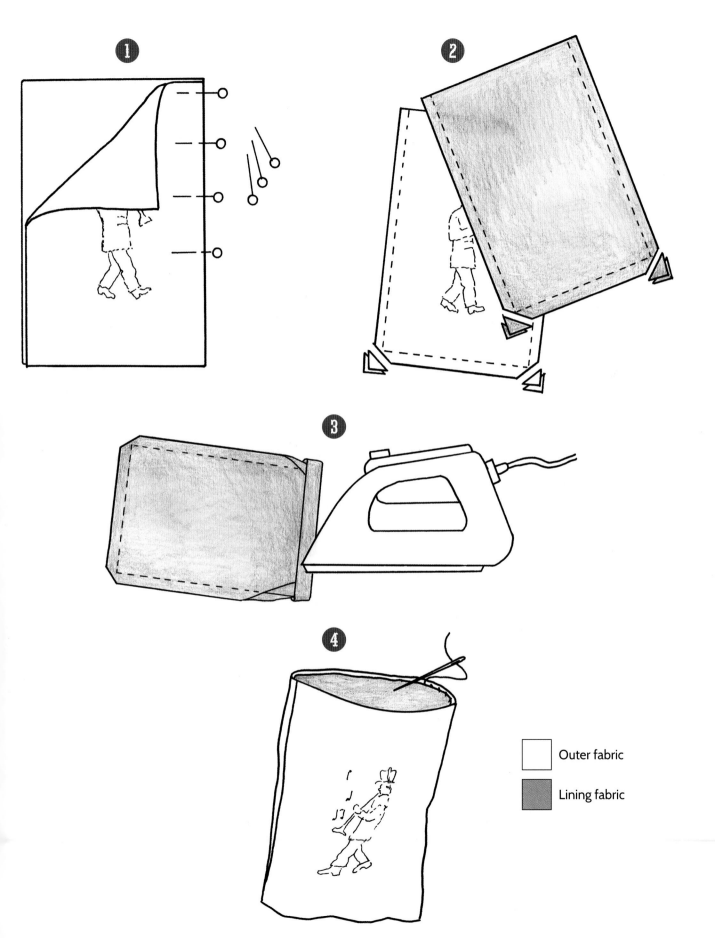

Outer fabric

Lining fabric

JUGGLING PENGUIN BIB

Make mealtimes — and party times — fun for your baby or toddler with a bib that is practical as well as pretty. Decorate it with a performing penguin juggling a trio of fish, and choose fabrics and binding tapes that are as colourful as possible.

YOU WILL NEED

★ Yellow printed cotton fabric, approximately
   10 x 6in (26 x 15cm)
★ Contrasting printed cotton fabric, approximately
   10in (26cm) square
★ White cotton or linen fabric, approximately
   16 x 10in (41 x 26cm), for backing and lining
★ DMC six-stranded embroidery thread in the following
   colours: 310 black, 444 golden yellow, 740 orange,
   794 cornflower, blanc
★ Sewing thread to match the binding
★ 8in (20cm) length of plain cotton bias binding,
   ⁵/₈in (1.5cm) wide
★ 48in (1.2m) length of patterned cotton bias binding,
   ⁵/₈in (1.5cm)
★ Basic embroidery kit (see pages 8–11)
★ 4in (10cm) embroidery hoop

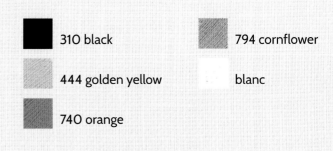

■ 310 black		▨ 794 cornflower
▨ 444 golden yellow		□ blanc
▨ 740 orange		

FINISHED SIZE

Approximately 9 x 7½in (23 x 19cm)

EMBROIDERING THE JUGGLING PENGUIN

Use two strands of embroidery thread throughout, unless otherwise stated.

On the yellow cotton fabric, using the template opposite enlarged by 150%, mark out the shape of the bib pocket with a water-soluble marker pen. Photocopy the penguin from page 34. Transfer it to the fabric (see page 12), placing it centrally within the drawn pocket outline. Place the fabric in a 4in (10cm) embroidery hoop.

Using 740 orange and satin stitch (see page 18), fill in the lower part of each wing, the beak and the feet. Fill in the top part of the chest with satin stitch using 444 golden yellow. Change to blanc and fill in the face and body in split stitch (see page 16). Use black to fill in the remaining areas of the head, body and wings in split stitch, and add two eyes with French knots (see page 19). Use 794 cornflower for the fish, filling in each shape with satin stitch.

Lastly, use a single strand of black to embroider the fish eyes using French knots. Outline any areas that need to be emphasized – such as underneath the belly and each side of the legs – using black thread and backstitch (see page 15). Outlining is particularly effective if you are using a very pale fabric where the white embroidery thread doesn't show up very clearly.

Remove the fabric from the hoop and wash out the erasable pen lines using cold water (see page 11). Leave to dry. Press on the reverse, following the pressing guidelines on page 11.

MAKING THE BIB

1 Cut out the embroidered piece along the lines you have drawn. This will form the pocket. Cut a piece of white fabric the same shape, to line the pocket. Photocopy the bib template opposite, enlarging it by 150%. Cut out one whole bib shape from the remaining white fabric and one from the contrasting printed cotton fabric.

2 Place the pocket and pocket lining wrong sides together and tack all round, then bind the straight edge using plain binding (see page 21). Place the main bib pieces wrong sides together and tack through both layers, close to the edge. Pin and tack the pocket to the main bib.

3 Bind the neck edge of the bib with patterned binding. Use the remaining binding to bind all round the outside edge of the bib, matching the centre of the length of binding to the centre point on the bottom of the bib.

4 The loose ends of the binding form the ties. Oversew (see page 20) the folded edges of the binding together, tucking in the raw edge on each end for a neat finish.

DID YOU KNOW?

A juggling penguin is a fun idea – but not very realistic. Animals were part of the circus from the early days. At first, they were just displayed in menageries, which are a kind of travelling zoo. People would pay to see strange, exotic creatures that they had only seen in books.

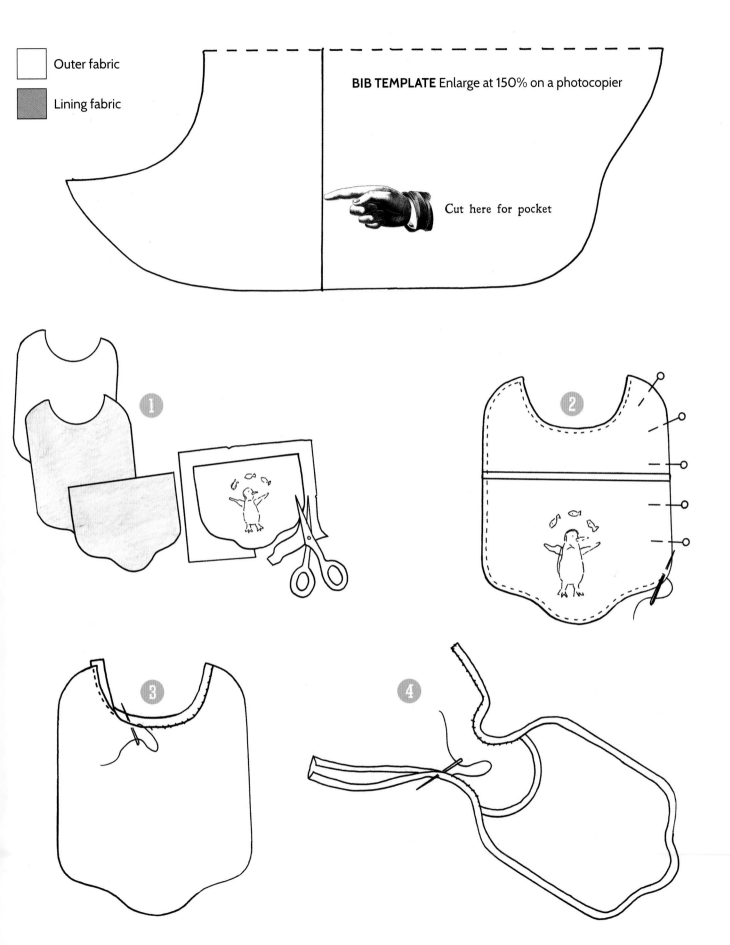

Outer fabric

Lining fabric

BIB TEMPLATE Enlarge at 150% on a photocopier

Cut here for pocket

BIG TOP CUSHION

Cheer up a living room, bedroom, nursery, conservatory, or maybe even a tent or a caravan, with this carnival cushion. Embroider a circus tent right at the centre, and make a striking patchwork border from an array of bright fabrics to frame it beautifully.

YOU WILL NEED

★ White cotton or linen fabric, at least 12in (30cm) square
★ Twelve 4¹/₈in (10.5cm) squares of fabric, all different, for the patchwork border
★ Plain or patterned fabric, 15 x 14in (38 x 36cm), for backing
★ DMC six-stranded embroidery thread in the following colours: 310 black, 444 golden yellow, 666 red, 703 grass green, 996 turquoise, blanc
★ Sewing thread to match the backing fabric
★ 12in (30cm) zip
★ Cushion pad, 14in (35cm) square
★ Basic embroidery kit (see pages 8–11)
★ 10in (25cm) embroidery hoop

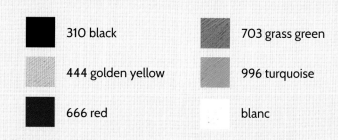

■	310 black	▨	703 grass green
▨	444 golden yellow	▨	996 turquoise
■	666 red	□	blanc

FINISHED SIZE

13¹/₂ x 13¹/₂in (34 x 34cm). The cushion pad is slightly larger than this, so you'll get a nice, plump cushion.

DID YOU KNOW?

The traditional large circus tent – or 'Big Top' – with its stripes of colourful canvas, dates back to mid-19th-century touring circuses.

EMBROIDERING THE BIG TOP DESIGN

Use two strands of embroidery thread throughout.

On white cotton or linen fabric, using a permanent pen, mark out a 7$\frac{1}{2}$in (19cm) square. Photocopy the Big Top motif from page 24, enlarging it so that it's approximately 3$\frac{1}{2}$–4in (9–10cm) high (see page 13). Photocopy the word 'circus' from page 92. Transfer these motifs onto your fabric using a water-erasable pen (see page 12). You can change the language, if you wish, and enlarge the lettering – just make sure that your whole design fits within the marked square with a margin of at least $\frac{3}{4}$in (2cm) all round. Place the fabric in a 10in (25cm) embroidery hoop.

Start with the Big Top. Using 310 black, fill in the entrance area in split stitch (see page 16). Using blanc, fill in the tent flaps on either side of the entrance and the row of small flags above the entrance, both in satin stitch (see page 18). Embroider the stripes on the tent in satin stitch, using 444 golden yellow and 666 red. Then embroider the stripes on the top of the tent using 996 turquoise, 666 red and blanc. Fill in the flag in satin stitch, using 703 grass green, 666 red and blanc. Use 703 grass green to embroider a line of stem stitch (see page 16) along the base of the tent. Then, using black, stitch the ropes and pegs in backstitch (see page 15).

For the lettering, use 444 golden yellow to fill in the small shapes within each letter in satin stitch. Then fill in the tops of the letters in 666 red and the bottoms of the letters in 996 turquoise, using split stitch.

Remove the fabric from the hoop and wash out the erasable pen lines using cold water (see page 11). Leave to dry. Press on the reverse, following the pressing guidelines on page 11. Cut out the square of fabric along the lines you have drawn.

MAKING THE CUSHION

1 For the patchwork border, cut out 12 squares of different fabrics, each measuring 4$\frac{1}{8}$in (10.5cm). With right sides together, taking a $\frac{3}{8}$in (1cm) seam allowance, stitch two squares together by hand or machine. Repeat to make a second pair. On each pair, press the seam to one side.

2 With right sides together, taking a $\frac{3}{8}$in (1cm) seam allowance, stitch one pair of squares to each side of the embroidered square. Press the seams to one side, away from the embroidered square.

3 Stitch the remaining squares together in two rows of four, using the same seam allowance. Press all the seams to one side. Join one strip to the top of the piece you have already made and one to the bottom. This completes the front panel of the cushion.

4 Cut the backing fabric into two pieces, each measuring 7$\frac{1}{2}$ x 14in (19 x 36cm). Fold $\frac{3}{8}$in (1cm) to the wrong side on one long edge of each piece. Place the zip right side up, then lay one backing piece right side up on top, with the folded edge as close to the zip teeth as possible, and pin in place. Repeat with the other backing piece on the other side of the zip with the other piece of backing fabric. Stitch in place by hand, or by machine using a zipper foot. Join the folded edges of fabric above and below the ends of the zip.

5 Open the zip halfway. Place the front and back panels of the cushion cover right sides together, aligning all the edges. (Trim the edges of the backing fabric, if necessary, so that it is the same size as the front panel.) Stitch together all round with a $\frac{3}{8}$in (1cm) seam allowance. Clip the corners, then turn the cover right side out through the gap in the zip. Press. Insert the cushion pad.

- Right side of fabric
- Wrong side of fabric

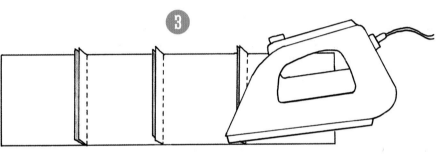

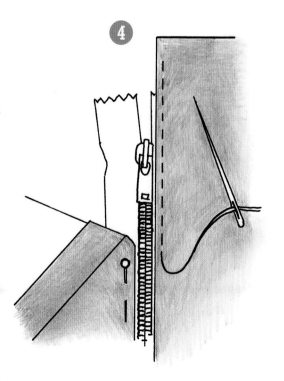

STEAM TRAIN CAKE BAND

This celebration cake with an embroidered band wrapped around is the perfect centrepiece for a circus-themed party. You can, of course, use any motifs from the book, but the circus train is a great choice as it fits so well on a long, narrow strip of fabric. Choo-choo! Here comes the circus!

YOU WILL NEED

★ White cotton or linen fabric, approximately 21¹/₂ x 6in (55 x 15cm)

★ Plain or printed cotton fabric, approximately 20 x 4in (50 x 10cm), for backing

★ DMC six-stranded embroidery thread in the following colours: 310 black, 648 grey, 676 honey, 725 yellow, 729 sandstone, 826 airforce blue, 892 deep coral, 911 emerald, 931 flint, 945 champagne, 977 light tan, 996 turquoise, 3768 slate grey, blanc

★ 30in (76cm) length of ribbon, 1³/₈in (35mm) wide

★ 40in (1m) folded edging braid, ³/₈in (1cm) wide

★ Thread to match the braid

★ 12 buttons (6 matching pairs), ³/₈in (9mm) in diameter

★ Basic embroidery kit (see pages 8–11)

★ 5in (12.5cm) embroidery hoop

■	310 black	▨	911 emerald
▨	648 grey	▨	931 flint
▨	676 honey	▨	945 champagne
▨	725 yellow	▨	977 light tan
▨	729 sandstone	▨	996 turquoise
▨	826 airforce blue	▨	3768 slate grey
▨	892 deep coral	□	blanc

FINISHED SIZE

3 x 19in (7.5 x 48cm), excluding ribbon

This band will fit a cake approximately 8in (20cm) in diameter. You can easily make your band shorter or longer, to fit any cake.

EMBROIDERING THE TRAIN DESIGN

Use two strands of embroidery thread throughout, unless otherwise stated.

On the rectangle of white cotton or linen fabric, using an erasable marker pen, draw a line along its length, about 1½in (4cm) below the centre; this will form the train track. Photocopy your chosen motifs – engine and carriages – and transfer them onto the fabric (see page 12), positioning them a little way above the line. Include the wheels of the engine but leave out any carriage wheels, as these will be represented by buttons.

Place the fabric in a 5in (12.5cm) embroidery hoop; using a hoop this size means that the area you are embroidering will fit inside but you will need to move the hoop from time to time, to complete the design.

Using the photo for reference, use 931 flint to fill in the funnel and the centres of the wheels in satin stitch (see page 18). Use 648 grey to stitch the wheels, with the stitches radiating out from the centre. Use 725 yellow, 892 deep coral, 911 emerald and 996 turquoise for the carriages, all in satin stitch. Still using satin stitch, fill in the star on the engine using 725 yellow, then fill in the other sections using 892 deep coral, 911 emerald and 826 airforce blue. Use 310 black for the coal. Use 945 champagne for the driver's face and 676 honey for the lion's body. Use 977 light tan for the driver's hair, the tiger's body and the lion's mane, and 729 sandstone for the camel. Complete the lion and tiger using blanc and 3768 slate grey and use the same grey to stitch the bars on the cages and the links between the carriages in split stitch. Use 911 emerald for the camel's harness.

To complete the embroidery, stitch the track in backstitch (see page 15), using 3768 slate grey. Stitch eyes and any other small details you wish to add, using a single strand of black and satin stitch or French knots (see page 19).

Remove the fabric from the hoop, and wash out the erasable pen lines using cold water. Leave to dry. Press on the reverse, following the pressing guidelines on page 11. Trim the fabric to 20 x 4in (50 x 10cm), ensuring that the train is in the centre of the strip.

MAKING THE CAKE BAND

1 Cut the ribbon in half so you have two pieces the same length. Trim one end of each ribbon into a 'V' to prevent fraying. Place the embroidered strip right side up, then pin the straight edges of the ribbons to the ends. Stitch in place by hand or machine.

2 Place the backing fabric on top, right side down. Stitch together along the two long sides by hand or machine, ⅜in (1cm) from the edges. Turn right side out.

3 Tuck in the raw edges of fabric at each end, to neaten. Cut the edging braid into two equal lengths. Pin one along the top edge of the band and one along the bottom edge, sandwiching the fabric inside the fold. Stitch in place.

4 Stitch the buttons firmly in place, two below each of the carriages, to represent wheels.

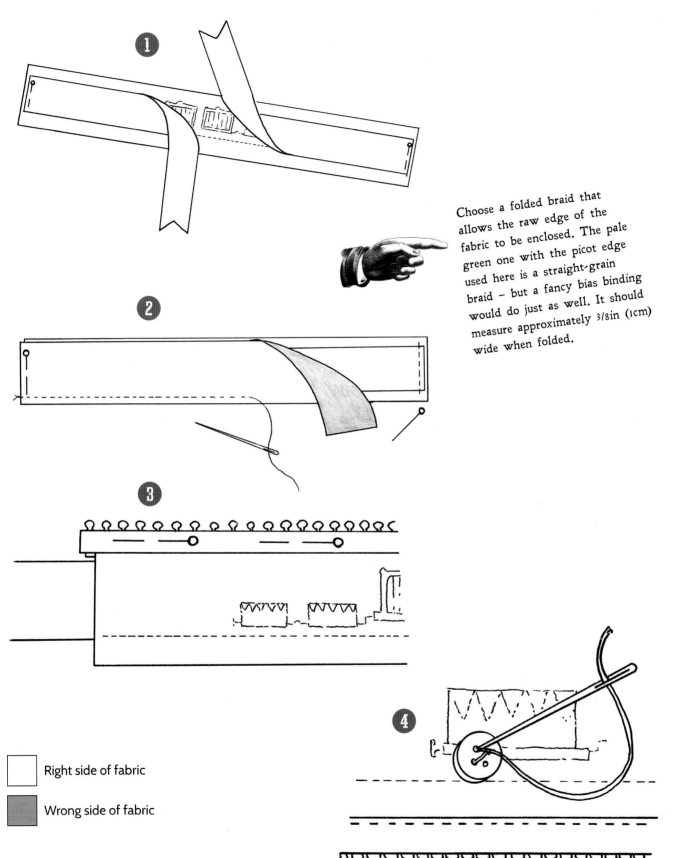

Choose a folded braid that allows the raw edge of the fabric to be enclosed. The pale green one with the picot edge used here is a straight-grain braid – but a fancy bias binding would do just as well. It should measure approximately 3/8in (1cm) wide when folded.

Right side of fabric

Wrong side of fabric

SHOW HORSE NEEDLE CASE

The compact design of a horse's head fits neatly on the front of this book-style needle case. With its rich embroidery and colourful plume, it would make a fine gift for someone who likes sewing and circuses.

YOU WILL NEED

- ★ White cotton or linen fabric, at least 8 x 6in (20 x 15cm)
- ★ Lining fabric, 7½ x 5½in (19 x 14cm)
- ★ Lightweight wadding, 7⅛ x 5⅛in (18 x 13cm)
- ★ Felt, 6⅜ x 4¾in (16 x 12cm)
- ★ DMC six-stranded embroidery thread in the following colours: 310 black, 444 golden yellow, 961 coral, 996 turquoise, 3689 shell pink, 3740 damson, 3755 pale blue, blanc
- ★ Sewing thread to match the fabric
- ★ 16in (40cm) length of narrow ribbon
- ★ Basic embroidery kit (see pages 8–11)
- ★ 6in (15cm) embroidery hoop

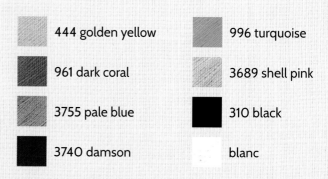

444 golden yellow		996 turquoise
961 dark coral		3689 shell pink
3755 pale blue		310 black
3740 damson		blanc

FINISHED SIZE

4¾ x 3⅛in (12 x 8cm)

EMBROIDERING THE HORSE MOTIF

Use two strands of embroidery thread throughout.

On white cotton or linen fabric, using a pencil or permanent marker pen, mark out a 7½ x 5½ in (19 x 14cm) rectangle and divide it in half. Do not cut it out at this stage. Photocopy the show horse motif from page 42, enlarging it to 4⅜in (11cm) (see page 13). Transfer it onto the fabric (see page 12), omitting the circular frame and instead drawing a straight line along the base of the neck. Place the fabric in a 6in (15cm) embroidery hoop; using a hoop this size means that the whole motif will fit inside the circle.

Using the photo for reference, use 444 golden yellow to embroider the rings on the bridle in satin stitch (see page 18). With 961 coral, embroider the straps on the bridle and harness in satin stitch. Using 3755 pale blue, embroider the horse's head and neck in split stitch (see page 16). The mane is filled using satin stitch and 3740 damson, and the feathers are also filled in satin stitch, radiating out from the centre line, using 996 turquoise and blanc. Embroider the lines on the feathers in split stitch, using 3755 pale blue. To complete the embroidery, fill the eye in blanc and 3740 damson, the ear centres in 3689 shell pink, and the nostril in 310 black, using satin stitch. Using a single strand of black, outline the eye and eyelashes in backstitch (see page 15).

Remove the fabric from the hoop and wash out the erasable pen lines using cold water (see page 11). Leave to dry. Press on the reverse, following the pressing guidelines on page 11.

MAKING THE NEEDLE CASE

1 Cut out the rectangle of fabric along the lines you have drawn. Cut the ribbon in half to give two 8in (20cm) lengths. Pin one ribbon to the centre of each side edge, on the right side of the embroidered piece.

2 Cut a rectangle the same size (7½ x 5½in 19 x 14cm) from lining fabric and a 7¼ x 5¼in (18 x 13cm) rectangle from lightweight wadding. Pin the two fabrics right sides together with the wadding centred on top.

3 Stitch all round by hand or machine, ⅜in (1cm) from the edges, leaving a 2¾in (7cm) gap on the lower edge. Clip the corners.

4 Turn right side out, fold the seam allowance to the inside on the opening, and slipstitch the folded edges together.

5 For the inside, cut a 6¼ x 4¾in (16 x 12cm) rectangle of felt. You can leave the edges plain, if you wish, or trim them with pinking shears. With the lining facing up, place the felt piece on top, in the centre. Stitch a line down the centre, through all thicknesses.

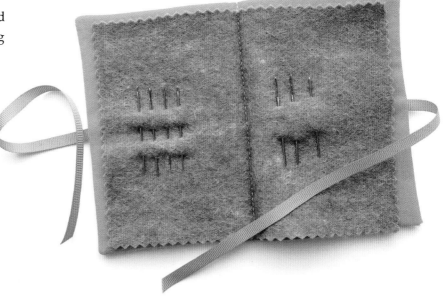

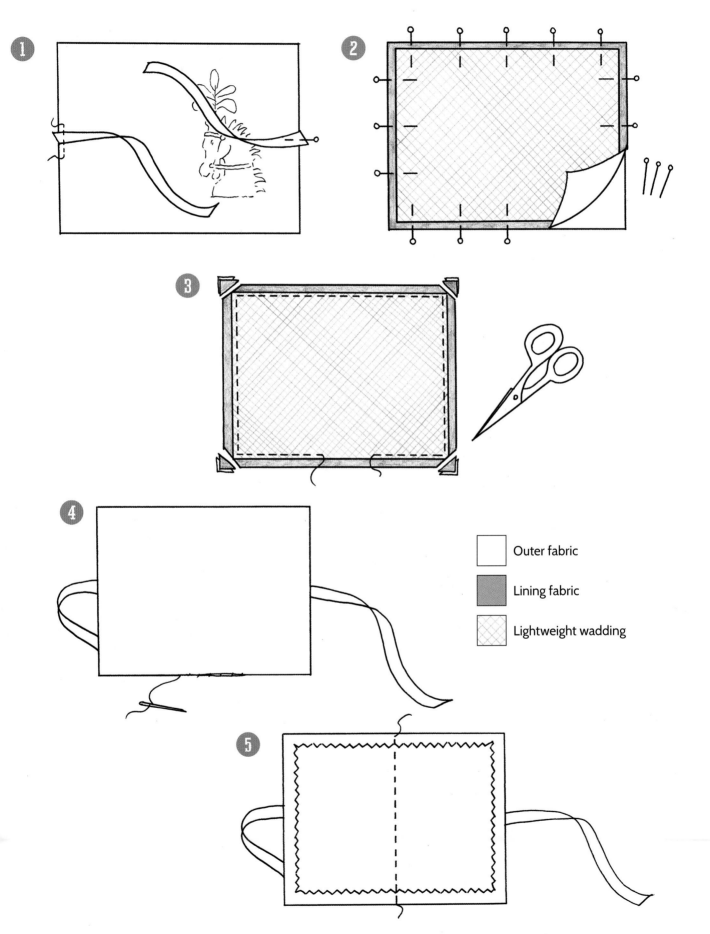

Outer fabric

Lining fabric

Lightweight wadding

SCROLLWORK BAG

A small cloth bag is a useful thing to carry in your pocket, ready for some impulse shopping. Or use it to carry a sketchbook, a tablet, your latest sewing project, toys — almost anything. The motif used here is a scrollwork pattern, typical of the kind of embellishment you see on circus signs and posters — but you could use any of the motifs from the book.

YOU WILL NEED

★ White cotton or linen fabric, approximately 12in (30cm) square
★ Printed cotton fabric, 14¼ x 10⅝in (36 x 27cm)
★ Plain cotton fabric, 20½ x 10⅝in (52 x 27cm), for lining
★ DMC six-stranded embroidery thread in the following colours: 602 rose pink, 444 golden yellow, 740 orange, 911 emerald, 3845 cyan
★ Sewing thread to match the fabric
★ 33in (84cm) cotton herringbone tape, 1in (2.5cm) wide
★ 33in (84cm) petersham ribbon, ⅝in (1.5cm) wide
★ Basic embroidery kit (see pages 8–11)
★ Embroidery hoop

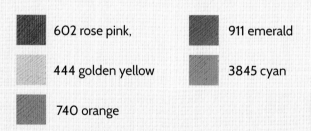

602 rose pink,

444 golden yellow

740 orange

911 emerald

3845 cyan

You can use a hoop of any size up to 7in (18cm). A large hoop will allow you to view the whole design; if you use a smaller hoop, you will need to move the fabric from time to time, as each section of the design is completed.

FINISHED SIZE

Approximately 10 x 10in (25 x 25cm)

EMBROIDERING THE SCROLLWORK

Use two strands of embroidery thread throughout.

On the white cotton, mark out a rectangle measuring 10⅝ x 7⅛in (27 x 18cm), using a pencil or a ballpoint pen. Photocopy the scroll motif from page 86 and a small star from page 82. Using a water-soluble marker pen, transfer them onto the fabric (see page 12), referring to the photo of the finished embroidery as a guide to placement. Place the fabric in an embroidery hoop.

Embroider the lines using chain stitch (see page 17) – two of the scrolls in 602 rose pink and the other two in 3845 cyan. Embroider the star in satin stitch (see page 18), using 444 golden yellow. Fill in the circles and small shapes in satin stitch, using 740 orange on the blue scrolls and 911 emerald on the pink scrolls.

Remove the fabric from the hoop and wash out the erasable pen lines using cold water (see page 11). Leave to dry. Press on the reverse, following the pressing guidelines on page 11.

 The central panel on this bag is the perfect blank canvas for any of the motifs in this book. Here one of the border designs from page 86 makes an attractive pattern repeat, but you could embroider a circus picture instead, or spell out a name or phrase using the alphabet letters from page 90.

MAKING THE BAG

1 Cut out the embroidered fabric rectangle along the lines you have drawn. Using a ⅜in (1cm) seam allowance throughout, stitch the two long edges of the embroidered fabric, which will form the centre front panel of the bag, to the two short edges of the printed cotton fabric, to form a tube. Join the two short edges of the lining fabric, also creating a tube.

2 Press the seams open, then press the bag so that the embroidered panel is in the centre front. Press the lining so that the seam is in the centre back. Stitch across the bottom of both the bag and the lining. Cut across the corners; this helps to reduce the bulk.

3 On the top edge of both the main bag and the lining, turn ⅜in (1cm) to the wrong side and press. Turn the main bag right side out.

4 Slip the lining inside the bag. To make the handles, place the petersham ribbon down the centre of the cotton tape and stitch it in place down both long edges. Cut it in half, to make two handles of equal length. Slip the ends of each handle between the bag and the lining and pin in place, lining up the edge of the handle on the bag front with the edge of the centre panel and using this to position the handle on the back of the bag. Slipstitch (see page 20) the lining to the bag along the folded edge, then topstitch (see page 21) all round the top of the bag, about ⅛in (3mm) from the edge.

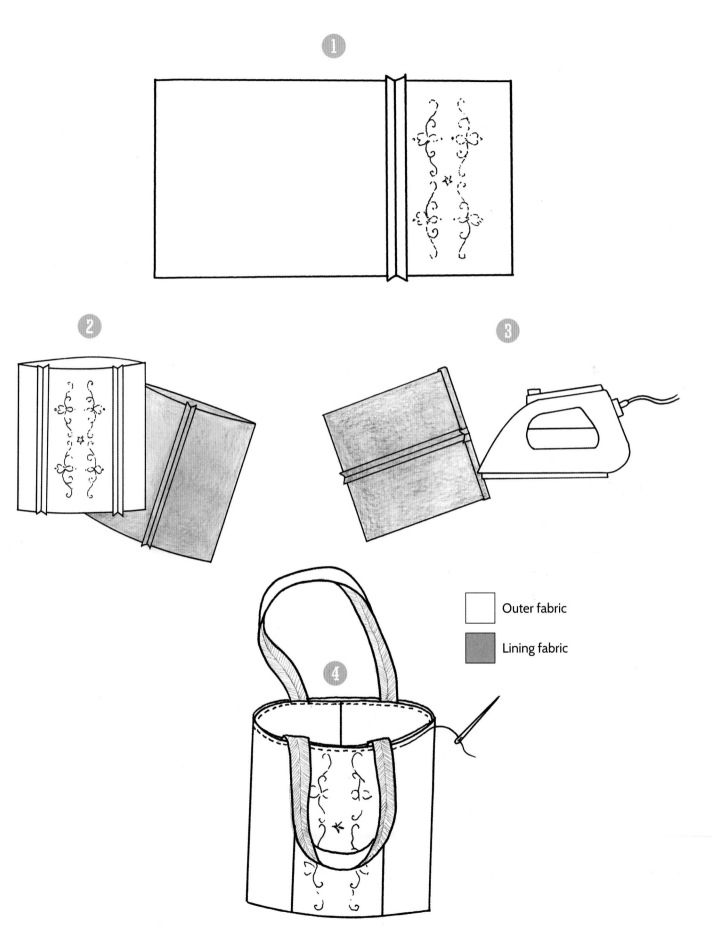

Outer fabric

Lining fabric

EMBROIDERY HOOP PICTURES

Here's a clever performing bear, standing upright and rolling a ball, ably assisted by two acrobats in baggy pants. The embroidery is made quick and easy by simply outlining the motifs. Embroidery hoops are an essential tool for keeping fabric taut as you sew. They also make a quick, easy and convenient way to display your handiwork, as demonstrated by this little trio of framed pictures.

YOU WILL NEED

★ Three pieces of white cotton or linen fabric, each approximately 10in (26cm) square
★ DMC six-stranded embroidery thread in the following colours: 300 chestnut, 550 purple, 666 red, 844 dark grey, 995 aqua
★ White sewing thread
★ 3yd (3m) cotton tape, ⁵⁄₈in (15mm) wide
★ 60in (1.5m) narrow striped ribbon, ³⁄₁₆in (5mm) wide
★ Basic embroidery kit (see pages 8–11)
★ Three 4in (10cm) embroidery hoops

	300 chestnut		844 dark grey
	550 purple		995 aqua
	666 red		

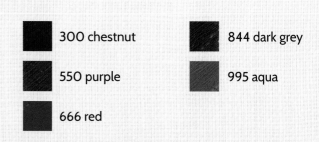

To bind the hoop, flat cotton tape, being quite soft and thin, is a good choice – but you could use ribbon instead.

FINISHED SIZE

4in (10cm) in diameter

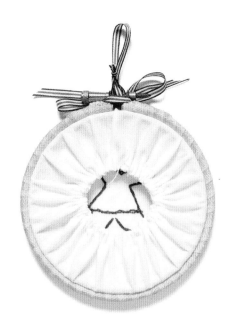

Use two strands of embroidery thread throughout. On each piece of white cotton or linen fabric, mark out a circle 9in (23cm) in diameter using a permanent pen. Photocopy two of the acrobats from page 54 and the bear with a ball from page 40. Transfer one motif onto each piece of fabric (see page 12), using a water-soluble pen and positioning each one centrally within the circle. Place each piece of fabric in a 4in (10cm) embroidery hoop.

For the acrobat with the bowler hat, embroider the outline in 844 dark grey, using split stitch (see page 16). Stitch the eye with two tiny straight stitches. On the wrong side, try not to move from one area of the design to another, or you may create strands across the white fabric that show through to the other side. Using 550 purple, outline the other acrobat in split stitch. Using 300 chestnut, outline the bear in split stitch, leaving the neck ruff unstitched, and outline the ball in 995 aqua. Fill in the ruff with 666 red, using satin stitch (see page 18). Use 300 chestnut to create the bear's eye, using a French knot (see page 19).

Remove each piece of fabric from its hoop and wash out the erasable pen lines using cold water (see page 11). Leave to dry. Press each piece on the reverse, following the pressing guidelines on page 11.

1 Bind the outer ring of each hoop with tape. To do this, secure one end of a 1yd (1m) length of tape to the metal plate below the screw fitting with a few stitches. You may find it useful to remove the screw before you do this. Wind the tape around the hoop, overlapping the edges slightly, until you reach the screw fitting on the other end. Trim off any excess tape and secure this end with a few stitches.

2 Cut out the fabric circle. Place it on top of the inner ring of the hoop and place the outer ring on top. Make sure that the embroidered motif is centred within the hoop and that the top of the motif is beneath the screw. Press the outer hoop down, then tighten the screw.

3 Using two strands of white sewing thread, work a line of running stitch around the edge of the fabric circle, about 1/8in (3mm) from the edge. Pull the thread ends to gather the fabric tightly, then fasten off securely.

4 For each picture, cut an 8in (20cm) length of narrow ribbon, tie the ends together, then push this loop under the screw to create a loop for hanging. Cut a 12in (30cm) length of narrow ribbon and tie this around the metal screw fitting and finish with a neat bow.

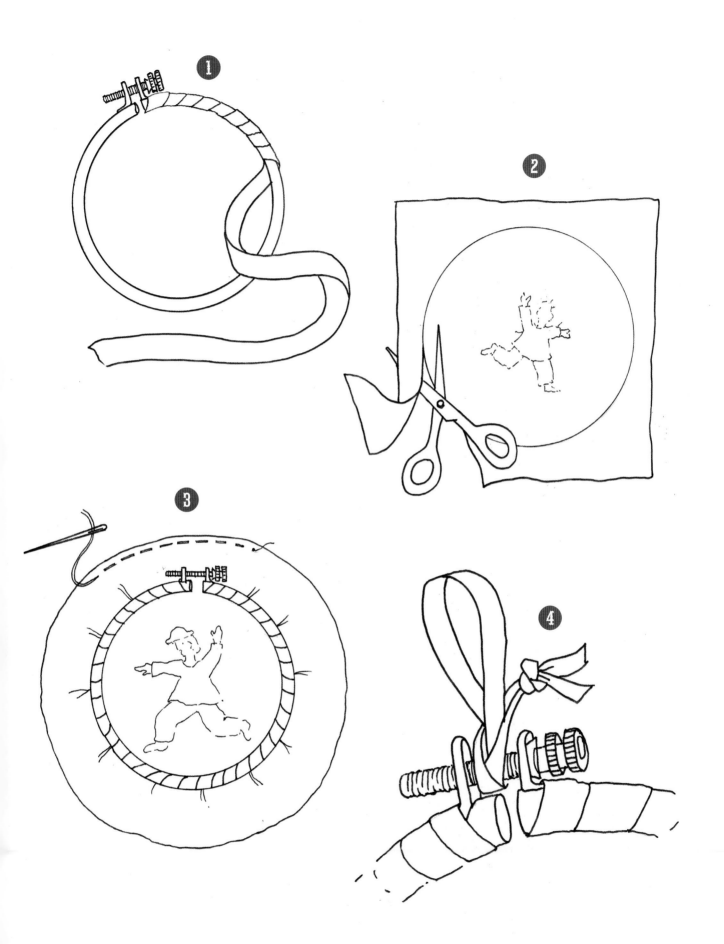

CIRCUS ANIMALS SHIRT

Embellish a plain shirt or dress with some playful circus animals.
Dogs can be trained to do all kinds of tricks and dog acts have long
been a family favourite in circuses. Children will find these cheeky
performing pooches delightful and you will have created a one-off
piece of clothing that is sure to become a family heirloom.

YOU WILL NEED

★ White cotton or linen shirt or dress in your desired size*
★ DMC six-stranded embroidery thread in the following colours: 310 black, 414 steel grey, 606 scarlet, 648 grey, 726 daffodil, 822 light beige, 892 deep coral, 894 sugar pink, 907 pistachio, 996 turquoise, blanc
★ Basic embroidery kit (see pages 8–11)
★ 5in (12cm) embroidery hoop

■	310 black	■	892 deep coral
■	414 steel grey	■	894 sugar pink
■	606 scarlet	■	907 pistachio
■	648 grey	■	996 turquoise
■	726 daffodil	□	blanc
■	822 light beige		

* Choose a garment with a flat yoke, to give you a good design area. Bear in mind that cotton and linen are easier to embroider than synthetic fabrics. If the garment is new, wash, dry and iron it before you start stitching, as this helps to soften the fabric.

FINISHED SIZE

The size shown is for a child aged 4–5 years.

EMBROIDERING THE DOGS

Use two strands of embroidery thread throughout.

Photocopy two dogs from page 36, enlarging them so that each one is about 3in (7.5cm) in both height and width. Check that the size is right for your garment: you may need to make your motifs smaller or larger, depending on the age of the child and the size of the garment (see page 13). Transfer the dogs onto your fabric (see page 12), positioning one on each side of the yoke. Place the fabric in a 5in (12cm) embroidery hoop so that one of the motifs in centred within the circle. When you are ready to embroider the other dog, move the hoop.

With 822 light beige, fill in each dog's body using split stitch (see page 16). Use 606 scarlet to fill in the noses in satin stitch (see page 18). Add a tiny highlight with a single small stitch in blanc on each nose. Add a few straight stitches in 894 sugar pink for the inner ears of the leaping dog. Use 907 pistachio and satin stitch for the other dog's ruff and for the top half of the hoop, then use 892 deep coral for the border of the standing dog's ruff, the pointed hat and the leaping dog's collar. For the ball and the base of the hoop, start by filling in the stars in 726 daffodil, using satin stitch, then fill in the rest in split stitch, using 996 turquoise. Use turquoise straight stitches radiating out from a central point for the pompom. Embroider the eyes in satin stitch using 310 black. Finally, use 648 grey and 414 steel grey to outline some of the areas, as you wish. Try using the lighter shade of grey around the ears and legs and the darker shade under the jawline, under each belly and down the edge of the hind legs.

Remove the fabric from the hoop and press on the reverse, following the pressing guidelines on page 11.

DECORATIVE DENIM JACKET

Arabesque borders and scrollwork are a decorative feature that you will see on circus posters, signs, props and scenery, and old-fashioned carnival rides. A classic denim jacket provides an excellent framework for showing them off with embroidery and colourful ric-rac braid.

YOU WILL NEED

★ Denim jacket in desired size*
★ DMC six-stranded embroidery thread in the following colours: 444 golden yellow, 666 red, 995 aqua, 996 turquoise
★ 1yd (90cm) ric-rac braid** in each of two colours
★ Basic embroidery kit (see pages 8–11)
★ 8in (20cm) embroidery hoop
★ Heat transfer pen
★ Thin white paper

444 golden yellow

666 red

995 aqua

996 turquoise

* Washed denim is soft and easy to embroider – so choose a well-worn jacket, or launder a new one before you start stitching.

**This amount of braid should be more than enough to fit across the back of the jacket – but do measure the width of the jacket before purchasing your braid.

FINISHED SIZE

The jacket shown here fits a child aged 8–10 years.

EMBROIDERING THE DESIGN

Use three strands of embroidery thread throughout.

Photocopy the border design from page 88 and the double star motif from page 82. Check that the size of the motifs is right for your garment. The jacket pictured here fits a child aged about 8–10 years: you may need to make your motifs smaller or larger, depending on the size of the jacket.

Use the heat transfer method (see page 12) to apply the design to your jacket, choosing a pen with an ink colour that will show up on the fabric, such as red or brown. Position the border design centrally on the back yoke and the star below the horizontal seam. Place the fabric in an 8in (20cm) embroidery hoop.

Use the picture of the finished jacket as a reference. On the border design, embroider the various small circles in satin stitch (see page 18), using 444 golden yellow, 666 red and 996 turquoise. On the central yellow circle, stitch a border of satin stitch all round, using red.

Stitch the horizontal line, the branching lines and two triangle shapes using chain stitch (see page 17) and 995 aqua. Use the same colour for the leaf shapes, filling these in with satin stitch. Using satin stitch, fill in the small triangles in 666 red and the remaining shapes in 996 turquoise.

For the star, use yellow to fill in the main shape in satin stitch. Embroider each point of the star separately, starting at the tip and working towards the centre. You may wish to fill in the shape with lines of running stitch (see page 15) before working satin stitch, to ensure that the thread covers the dark fabric adequately (see page 15). Fill in the other star points using 666 red. Remove the fabric from the hoop and press on the reverse, following the pressing guidelines on page 11.

Pin lines of ric-rac braid along the seamline and just below. Using a single strand of embroidery thread to match the braid, stitch it in place, using slipstitch (see page 20), attaching both wavy edges to the fabric.

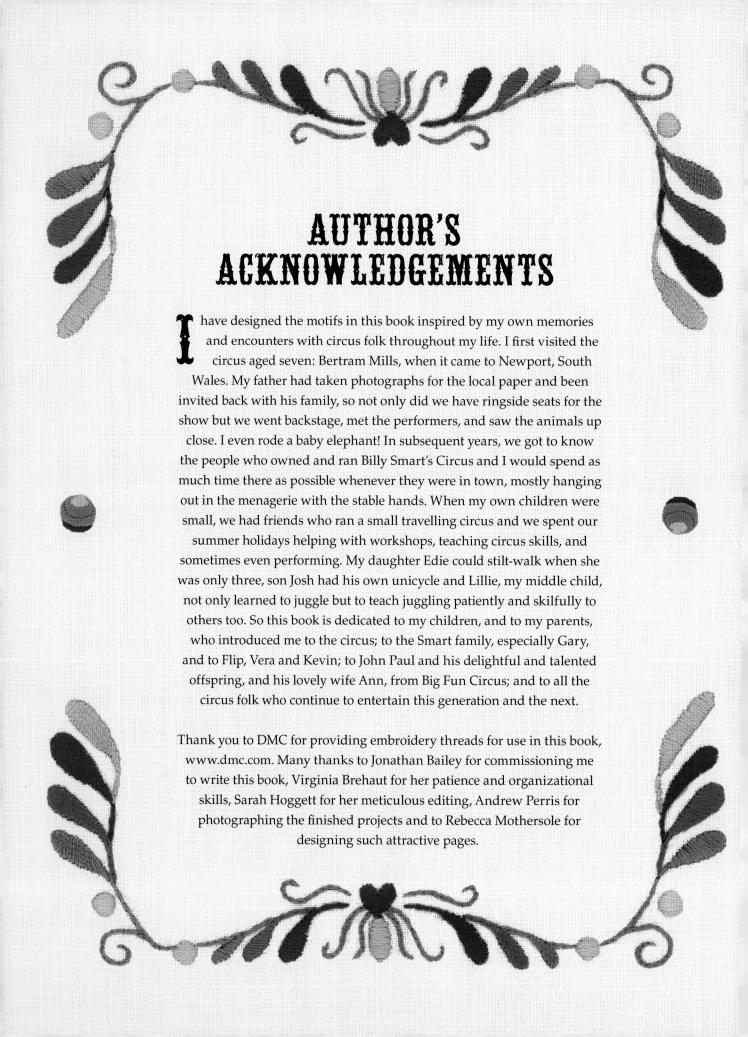

AUTHOR'S ACKNOWLEDGEMENTS

I have designed the motifs in this book inspired by my own memories and encounters with circus folk throughout my life. I first visited the circus aged seven: Bertram Mills, when it came to Newport, South Wales. My father had taken photographs for the local paper and been invited back with his family, so not only did we have ringside seats for the show but we went backstage, met the performers, and saw the animals up close. I even rode a baby elephant! In subsequent years, we got to know the people who owned and ran Billy Smart's Circus and I would spend as much time there as possible whenever they were in town, mostly hanging out in the menagerie with the stable hands. When my own children were small, we had friends who ran a small travelling circus and we spent our summer holidays helping with workshops, teaching circus skills, and sometimes even performing. My daughter Edie could stilt-walk when she was only three, son Josh had his own unicycle and Lillie, my middle child, not only learned to juggle but to teach juggling patiently and skilfully to others too. So this book is dedicated to my children, and to my parents, who introduced me to the circus; to the Smart family, especially Gary, and to Flip, Vera and Kevin; to John Paul and his delightful and talented offspring, and his lovely wife Ann, from Big Fun Circus; and to all the circus folk who continue to entertain this generation and the next.

Thank you to DMC for providing embroidery threads for use in this book, www.dmc.com. Many thanks to Jonathan Bailey for commissioning me to write this book, Virginia Brehaut for her patience and organizational skills, Sarah Hoggett for her meticulous editing, Andrew Perris for photographing the finished projects and to Rebecca Mothersole for designing such attractive pages.

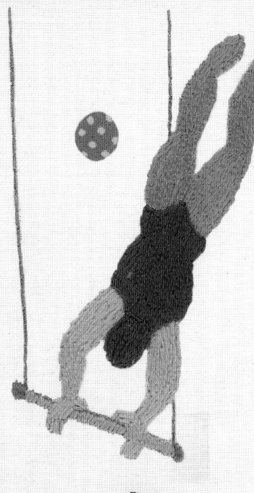

First published 2020 by
Guild of Master Craftsman Publications Ltd
Castle Place, 166 High Street, Lewes,
East Sussex, BN7 1XU

Text © Susie Johns, 2020
Copyright in the Work ©
GMC Publications Ltd, 2020

ISBN 978 1 78494 547 3

Publisher Jonathan Bailey
Production Jim Bulley, Jo Pallett
Senior Project Editor Virginia Brehaut
Editor Sarah Hoggett
Managing Art Editor Gilda Pacitti
Art Editor Rebecca Mothersole

Colour origination by GMC Reprographics
Printed and bound in China

To place an order, or to request a catalogue, contact: GMC Publications Ltd, Castle Place,
166 High Street, Lewes, East Sussex, BN7 1XU, United Kingdom Tel: +44 (0)1273 488005
www.gmcbooks.com